SELECTED POEMS OF *Jorge Carrera Andrade*

Jorge Carrera Andrade

SELECTED POEMS OF

Jorge Carrera Andrade

TRANSLATED AND WITH AN

INTRODUCTION BY

H. R. Hays

State University of New York Press
ALBANY
1972

*Assistance for the translation of this volume
was given by the Center for Inter-American Relations*

Selected Poems of Jorge Carrera Andrade

First edition

Published by State University of New York Press,
99 Washington Avenue, Albany, New York 12210
Translation © 1972 State University of New York

Printed in
the United States
of America
Designed by Raymond A. Grimaila

Library of Congress Cataloging in Publication Data

Carrera Andrade, Jorge, 1903-
Selected poems of Jorge Carrera Andrade.

English and Spanish.
PQ 8219.C27A6 1972   861   72-161498
ISBN 0-87395-067-4
ISBN 0-87395-167-0 (microfiche)

mw

Contents

v

INTRODUCTION

On a windy dusty day in August 1912, at the age of nine, Jorge Carrera Andrade and his young brother were walking in the market in Quito accompanied by a servant girl when their ears were assailed by gunfire.

People began to run, screaming, "The militia from the north are coming," "The artillery has gone over!," "The police are firing on the people!," "They say the president's been arrested!"

The children and their nurse ran home at top speed. This was the poet's introduction to the instability of Ecuadorian government and to the struggle between the liberal elements in the country and the oligarchy of rich landowners, a struggle which is still not resolved. Carrera's first brush with revolution turned out to be the fall of General Eloy Alfaro, considered to be a liberal. Later the boy was to be a witness to the president's assassination as he was driven through the streets, a prisoner.

The political and social struggles which have gone on in Carrera Andrade's native country have had much to do with shaping his career, his poetic material and his attitude toward life. The poet, born in 1903, is the son of a liberal lawyer, later to become a judge of the supreme court, who was famous for defending the rights of the Indians against the landowners. The family owned a large house in Quito and also a *quinta* or country estate which included a farm, livestock, and a large garden. It was here that he came to know the Indian farm workers and developed a sympathy for the Ecuadorian people.

He was educated in private schools and by the time he reached the equivalent of high school, he was a member of a literary club and at age fifteen he was editing a literary review.

The university brought a deepening involvement in social protest and, eventually revolutionary activity. World War I had resulted in the Russian Revolution which had repercussions even in Quito, where Marxism was discussed as was the Mexican Revolution. It was a period in which an unleashing of social optimism took place. From the point of view of the present, this was the beginning of the "evolution of rising expectations" during which the oppressed peoples all over the world developed a new consciousness and a new determination.

The student groups in Quito, as so often has been the case in Latin America, reacted most strongly to the currents of the times and began to organize politically. In Ecuador in that era there were no unions; the majority of the population consisted (and still consists) of illiterate Indian agricultural workers exploited by a hereditary landowning class which stemmed from the Spanish conquerors. The students raised the slogan, "Bread, Land, and Literacy," which, of course, is still appropriate as a rallying cry for many parts of southern continent.

Carrera's first book, *Estanque inefable*, was published in 1922 and he joined with the students who were trying to make contact with nearby Indians in order to educate them politically. The young missionaries made little progress for the workers were too much under the influence of a reactionary parish priest. The workers of Guayaquil, however, were dissatisfied with the financial policies of President José Luis Tamayo and demanded that he check the runaway speculation which was raising the cost of living. The landowners, as usual, merely wanted the people repressed. Carrera Andrade, as his contribution to the revolution, busied himself with editing and printing an underground sheet, *Humanidad*.

Acting on a premature message heralding an uprising, a group of students, including the poet, gathered outside the Teatro Sucre only to be pounced upon by the police. Carrera spent his first night in jail in solitary confinement.

Agitation went on until the next presidential election. Unfortunately the candidate of the left, Juan Manuel Lasso, lost to a middle of the road candidate, Dr. Gonzalo Cordoba. The later soon fell ill; political trickery was suspected; a group of military arrested him and handed over the government to a committee of seven private citizens who immediately took measures to improve the economy of the country. Eventually Isidro Ayora was installed as president. When he soon turned to the right the young people renewed the struggle against the Establishment. Carrera Andrade became General Secretary of the newly formed Social Party, at the same time working for the Department of Education.

Partly because the government was beginning to look askance at his activities and partly because the socialists wished to form international connections, he was chosen as a delegate to the Fifth International Congress in Moscow. Unfortunately funds for the expenses of the trip were merely promised and Carrera had to pay his own way. Because of intrigues in the Ecuadorian party, no money was ever forthcoming with the result that the poet worked his way through Europe, selling hearing aids in Germany, and doing editorial jobs in Marseilles. He never reached Moscow but in Paris he met the Peruvian political leader Haya de la Torre and, briefly the poet, César Vallejo. Later the Chilean, Gabriela Mistral, was to give him shelter for a time in her villa in Avignon. In Barcelona he got work with a publishing house and in the spring of 1933 contributed to a review, *Hoja Literaria*.

These were formative years in which the young Ecuadorian acquired a cosmopolitan outlook. His graduate school was Europe whose traditions both attracted and repelled and made him more acutely aware of those values he felt were characteristic of the New World.

Carrera Andrade returned to his native country in 1933 to find himself in the midst of a new uproar. He became secretary of the senate while the legislature mounted a violent attack against the president, Martinez Mera. The leader of the revolt was José Maria Velasco Ibarra, destined to become president five times (and just expelled from that office). In Carrera's view he has a record of demagogy. In 1934 he invoked Stalin and Mussolini alternately and developed a style of oratory aimed at arousing the masses in his pursuit of the highest office.

Carrera Andrade wrote the manifesto for a new group, a Social-Agrarian Party and presently it became his duty, as secretary of the senate to announce to Martinez Mera that he had been deposed by the congress. In the election which followed Carrera supported the Social-Agrarian, Zambrano Orejuela, but Valasco Ibarra became a candidate and succeeded in obtaining a majority. Carrera Andrade was appointed consul in Paita, Peru. This was the beginning of a diplomatic career which the poet was to pursue for the rest of his life. He accepted the post mainly because the socialists were split, the new party had not prospered, and liberalism seemed, at the time, to have no future. On the other hand it was obviously to Velaseo Ibarra's advantage to keep him out of the country.

In the years that followed the poet was consul at Le Havre and finally became Consul General of Japan, a post which he held for three years. The aesthetic side of Japanese culture and Zen philosophy attracted him, as is attested by several poems written during this period. He was also aware of the military buildup for enigmatic episodes involving the Japanese secret police warned him that the country was a prey to tensions which were leading to the tragic adventure of Pearl Harbor.

Carrera Andrade did not spend the war years in Japan, for in 1940 he was transferred to the Ecuadorian consulate in San Francisco. His arrival in the United States coincided with a new interest in Latin American literature, President Roosevelt's policy was one of rapprochement with the southern continent. Government subsidy was even available for the translation of poetry. For the first time North Americans began to be aware of the poetic riches of Latin American literature. Carrera's work had already been translated into French. Now Muna Lee translated a group of his poems into English in *Secret Country*, published in 1946, and his poems also appeared in H.R. Hays' *12 Spanish American Poets* in 1943 and in the government-sponsored *Anthology of Contemporary Latin American poetry*, edited by Dudley Fitts and published in 1947. Meanwhile Carrera's work, to 1940, was collected and published in *Registro del Mundo* in Quito.

In 1944 another revolution triggered by a general strike ousted President Arroyo del Rio. Hopes of real reform were dashed when the ubiquitous Velasco Ibarra was recalled from exile and installed as president. The new foreign minister shifted Carrera Andrade to the position of chargé d'affaires in Venezuela. While in this country the poet worked for closer relations between Venezuela, Ecuador, and Colombia. In an undeclared war over a boundary dispute, Peru had in 1942 taken over the Ecuadorian province which borders on the Amazon. The U.S., Argentina, and Brazil arbitrated the dispute but the treaty which resulted, leaving Peru the disputed province, created dissatisfaction in Ecuador which has never subsided. Carrera endeavored to recruit Latin American sentiment in favor of a restitution of this lost province.

By 1946 Valasco Ibarra had exiled the president of the congress and performed other unconstitutional acts. In protest Carrera Andrade resigned. He remained in Venezuela using his freedom from government employment to produce prose works and to publish his selected poems with a preface by the Spanish poet Pedro Salinas (Caracas, 1946).

In 1947 Valasco Ibarra's dictatorial behavior caused his removal by the army. A liberal coalition in congress appointed Arosema Tola president. Carrera, who was back in Quito,

xiii

during the selection of a chief executive worked for a compromise between the liberals and conservatives and had supported Arosema Tola. The new government sent the poet to England to deal with Ecuador's British debt with the title of Envoy Extraordinary and Plenipotentiary Minister. He had begun to negotiate for the exportation of rice to pay off the debt when an election at home brought the liberal, Galo Plaza, into power.

The poet returned in 1948 to Quito to face the death of his father, a divorce from his wife, and difficulties in his diplomatic career. The president had appointed a Chancellor unfriendly to Carrera Andrade who, therefore, for the time being again retired into private life. He became vice president of the Casa de la Cultura and set about improving its periodical. A year later he was designated a delegate to Unesco a position which took him back to Paris where he presently became editor of the Spanish publications of that organization. By 1952 a new electoral triumph for Velasco Ibarra, who always came in as a radical and departed as a reactionary, meant that the poet would continue more or less in exile for the next four year period. While in France he embarked on his three-volume history of Ecuador. *The Way of the Sun*, *The Evergreen Land*, and *Gallery of Insurgents and Mystics*. The first two were completed and published by 1955.

In general, Carrera Andrade had arrived at a philosophy of stoicism. Politically his experience of revolutions and coups had been frustrating. The patient self-contained Indians of his native land, however, and the visual beauty of its snow-capped peaks and green valleys became for him a symbol of innocence and simplicity which he cherished during periods in which he felt overwhelmed by the cynicism and materialism of the world of highly developed technology.

During a short stay with a relative on Long Island where he underwent medical treatment for a nervous illness, Carrera, while attending a conference at the U.N., was approached with the offer of a special mission to Chile and Brazil to discuss the always painful matter of the 1942 treaty with Peru which Ecuador still felt to be unjust. The president who made this offer was Velasco Ibarra, elected in 1960 for the fourth time. After something of a rapprochement and a personal interview with the old political magician, Carrera accepted the task for the issue was one he had always championed.

When he returned home, he was named ambassador to Venezuela. This was during the disturbed administration of Rómulo Betancourt. The latter had been democratically elected in 1959 after the country had submitted to some years of dictatorial rule by Delegado Chalbaud and after him Pérez Jiménez, both colonels who came to power by a coup. Betancourt had a liberal party, the Accion Democrática, behind him but by now Cuba had had its revolution and the communist left was in no mood to accept cautious reforms. Stimulated by Castro, a guerilla organization, the F.A.L.N. undertook actions aimed at unseating the Betancourt government. It was nothing out of the ordinary to hear gunfire at night and once the Ecuadorian embassy was almost in the line of fire as guerrillas from the mountains aimed a fusillade at the residence where Betancourt, they erroneously supposed, was staying. Betancourt had already been the object of a terrorist attack in 1960 when henchmen of the dictator, Trujillo, flung a dynamite-laden radio-controlled car against his limousine. When Carrera Andrade was presented to him, the scars on his hands were still visible.

Carrera, who was personally friendly with Betancourt, made the embassy a literary center, resuming amicable relations with the Venezuelans he knew from his former visit. Meanwhile Velasco Ibarra, up to his old tricks, had imprisoned the president of the Ecuadorian congress. The air force supported the leader of congress with the result that Velasco Ibarra was once more deposed and a new executive, Arosemena Monroy was appointed by congress. The new president seconded Carrera's efforts at cementing relationships between Ecuador and her neighbors by visiting Venezuela officially.

However, by July 1963, the army once more intervened and deposed Arosema Monroy. Venezuela suspended relations and the poet was once again without government employment. Ecuador, for the time being, was governed by an army junta.

On the poet's return to Quito he found that the anti-communism of the junta was such that even socialists were looked upon with a cold eye. Actually both socialists and communists were at this time fractured into small, inefficient splinter groups. After some months of inactivity, Carrera Andrade was designated embassador to Nicaragua. From here he was transferred to Paris as ambassador to France in 1964 and in 1966 as a delegate to the Unesco conference. In the same year, when the legislature had named Arosema Gomez interim president, the latter called Carrera Andrade home to become Minister of Foreign Affairs. Six months later the poet resigned to busy himself with prose essays collected as *Interpretations of Hispano-America*. In 1967 Arosemena Gomez appointed him ambassador to the Netherlands. The situation in his own country was dubious for an election was coming up in which Velasco Ibarra was a candidate. While he was in Holland the review, *Norte*, dedicated a special number (3 and 4, 1968) to Carreras poetry. In the election that same year, however, Velasco Ibarra, by a small margin, was for the fifth time voted into the highest office. During other administrations he had been held in check by the army; this time he had the support of the army and the reactionary establishment. Realizing that Velasco Ibarra meant to proclaim himself dictator, Carrera resigned his ambassadorship and returned to France, in September on 1968, where he remained, for he was warned by the adherents of Ibarra that he would not be welcome in Ecuador.

He worked as Revisor of the Spanish translation department of Unesco and began his autobiography, subsequently published in Puebla, Mexico (1970). He also began a long poem, "The Book of Exile." In June 1968 he came to the

International Poetry Conference at the State University of New York at Stony Brook. This led to a two-year appointment to teach Spanish-American Literature at Stony Brook, ending in 1971. While in the United States, he has read at Vassar College, at Harvard College, and also at the International Festival of Poetry at the Library of Congress in Washington.

This brief biographical sketch is enough to indicate Jorge Carrera Andrade's humanitarian beliefs, his cosmopolitan career and his lifelong connection with politics. Although his long service abroad and periods of exile have much of the time kept him from participating directly in cultural activities in Quito, he has never lost contact with Ecuadorian poetry and the leading writers of his country have always recognized the value of his work and seen to it that it was published in his native land. During his residence in countless foreign countries he has met nearly everyone of cultural importance in the Latin World as well as many English and French writers. His reputation is already established in France, England, Holland, Italy, and in the republics of Central and South America.

Like other Latin American poets of his generation, he started writing with a background of "modernismo" as the neo-symbolist movement was called in the southern continent. Latin American literary culture in the nineteenth century, after the independence movement, drew much of its inspiration from France. Under the leadership of the famous Nicaraguan, Rubén Dario (1867-1916), it achieved its own voice but it still clung to traditional literary images and, reacting to the spiritual poverty of the social scene, took refuge in exotic subjects: oriental splendor, myths of the conquistadores, Scandinavian mythology, nymphs, centaurs, peacocks, and above all swans, abounded as the spirit of romanticism still flourished, variously costumed.

It was the second wave of modernist verse, descibed as "mundonovismo" which constituted a rebellion against literary clichés and Verlainian melancholy. The Mexican Enrique

Gonzalez Martinez in 1915 published his book *The Death of the Swan* containing the famous sonnet which became a kind of manifesto.

> Then wring the neck of this delusive swan,
> White note upon the fount's blue overflow
> That drifts in feathered grace and can not know
> The essence of the world, the voice of tree and stone.

The young poets of the twentieth century called for direct observation; the landscape and the Indian began to be discovered as in the work of the Mexican Ramon López Velarde and Luis Carlos López of Colombia, instead of turning away from the grimness of provincial life, made use of it in order to produce scathing satirical humor.

Carrera Andrade, as he himself tells us, came in contact with French poetry very early in life. He had his Baudelairian phase and later something of Francis Jammes' gentle, open-eyed wonder at the world left its impression on his writing. While still a schoolboy he encountered the vigorous experimentalism of Guillaume Apollinai. e.

Although he was aware of the surrealists and, later in life personally friendly with some of them, the movement did not impress him as it did César Vallejo and Pablo Neruda. The latter was also to find inspiration in Walt Whitman but it is not until the last decade that we find something of Whitman in the poetry of Carrera Andrade.

One more current in Spanish writing, that of "ultraism" a movement parallel to surrealism, initiated in Madrid in 1918 by Guillermo de la Torre and Cansino Asséns, relates to Carrera's development. The ultraists stressed the metaphor, seeking fresh and unsual comparisons. The catual movement was short-lived but Carrera took the metaphor, as Pedro Salinas points out, and made it his basic unit of composition. It is the means by which the poet's personal vision unifies and takes possession of the objects of his environment. Certain recurring metaphors also function as symbols and set the tone of his lyricism. His metaphors are not strained or obscure, they unroll in luxurious profusion with the spontaneity of birdsong.

Salinas has called him a poet of "seeing" and indeed a great deal of his early work stems from the visual. Other senses, however, contribute to his elegant sensualism. For instance, "The Song of the Apple":

> Miniature evening sky;
> Yellow, green, flesh color
> With stars of sugar
> Cloudlets of satin.

vision, taste and touch all combine to intensify the evocation of the familiar fruit. It is this loyalty to the sensuous world which relates Carrera to the North American imagists, themselves descendents of the symbolists. While the northern poets on the whole used the metaphor sparingly, they, too, culturated the sensuous image to suggest and imply, avoiding too explicit statement.

Compare William Carlos Williams:

> The alphabet of the trees
> is fading in the
> song of the leaves...

with the following from Carrera's beautiful spring song:

> The almond tree buys a dress
> To take its first communion. The sparrows
> Announce their green merchandise in doorways.

Or the famous Pound metro poem:

> The apparition of these faces in the crowd;
> Petals on a wet, black bough.

It is the precision of observation plus the bringing together of similarities and dissonances not used before which makes such metaphors emotionally effective.

Salinas makes much of the window as a recurring image and symbol in Carrera's work. He quotes a number of passages which stress the window as the poet's "major property", as "invitation to the journey," as "a niche opened in the sky." The window becomes equated with the eye and relates to the traveller who is both the inquiring observer and the exile.

"The window," says Salinas, "is a subtle deception, a fallacious form of possession and dominion over the exterior world through human will."

Thus the traveller owns fleetingly only what he sees and by extension is a symbol of every human being who passes through life unable to keep anything, feeling himself to be a spectator.

Carrera's self-acknowledged stoicism, therefore, can be equated with the existential philosophy of our time, the belief that an acceptance of the transitory is the only strategy for enduring the human condition. In specific terms the poet's own life reflects a turning away from action to contemplation and interpretation, the young activist gives way to the poet.

There are several other facets to Carrera's work and one of these is the interpretation and evocation of the Indian, a direction which some of the Peruvian poets for a time entitled "indigenismo" and tried to raise to the level of a school.

The exploration and exaltation of the Indian heritage of Central and South America was best publicized by the Mexican murals of the 1920. The preoccupation was more than one of local color. In the countries of the Andes and in Mexico and Guatemala, the gulf between the man of Indian blood and the Spanish conqueror could be compared to that between the blacks and the whites in the United States. There are two difference, however: in Central America and in the Andes the Indians constitute the majority of the population and often do not even speak the language of their exploiters. The cultural revolutionaries of the 1920 s were doing two things, upholding the rights of the most exploited group and asserting that mestization was inevitable. From this it followed that the Indian heritage was of the greatest importance. Just as the American black has found it necessary to assert and himself believe that "black is beautiful," so the indigenists had to lift the Indian from the position of despised pariah and workhorse to a status in which his past culture was recognized as rivalling that of the ancient European world.

Carrera's early indigenist poems were written in the 1920 s and constitute a marriage between his fluency of metaphor and local color.

> The horseman carries a roll of wind
> In the wing of his poncho...

or

> The men from the commune carry the morning
> Caught in the teeth of their sickles...

Most of these poems tend to be decorative but in "The Uprising" he chronicles one of those local revolts in which the campesinos try to take possession of land denied them and are shot down by the soldiers. Here he is touching on one of the burning issues of Indian life, the need to own their own land. Agrarian reform is a necessity which is now being carried out in Peru and still needs to be completed in Ecuador.

This particular poem is significant as a link between indigenismo and social protest. In the volume, *Tiempo Manual*, and elsewhere there are poems with explicit social content. It is significant that three major Latin American poets have all drawn inspiration from their social convictions and each transmuted it into poetry in a different way. Neruda is the most propagandistic, even though his satire on the exploiters is brilliantly surrealistic. Vallejo's social expression was a kind of extending of his own tragic emotion into a universal passion for justice. Carrera Andrade has always been torn between his acute appreciation of the beauty of the natural world and man's failure to live up to it.

> There is something more than methods, systems and
>   doctrines:
> Free air, free light, free water,
> The profile of the voice traced by echo,
> The uprising of the vegetables against Political Economy.
> Nakedness, dreams, fine weather, laughter
> And the moon just out of the oven
> Distributed among all men yet always whole.

The doctrinaire Marxist has always insisted that culture and subjective aesthetic values must take second place, that the "superstructure" is always inferior in importance to the hard facts of economics and material deprivation. Carrera, a poet of strong social conviction can insist:

> The right to love and walk everywhere are not ours,
> We are slavetraders in our own lives.

but he also tells us:

> You are right, workman cicada,
> To mine the state with your profound song.
> Comrade, the two of us form the extreme left of this
>   world.

Even in the songs of social protest he does not abandon the brilliant hues of his metaphors and his perception that the profit system is not the whole story. This last, indeed, is not far from what the younger generation is saying.

Carrera's poetry of the 1950s and 1960s, collected in *Poesia Ultima* (New York, 1968) continues to deal with his familiar themes but in new ways. Indigenismo, for instance, is reinforced by this historical studies and thus Ecuador's past becomes the source of a long poem which reveals a more or less epical intention. "The Peacemaker" uses Pedro de la Gasca as a symbol of positive values. He is a cleric, sent by Spain to put an end to Pizarro's dictatorial usurpation of the empire of the Andes. As a man of peace who vanquishes the cruel adventurer without bloodshed, he stands for humanitarian values while the conquerer is intended as an image of authoritarianism. While it is true that Gasca represents the best elements in Spanish culture, nevertheless, he, too, represents the conquest which, from the Indian point of view, was illigitimate. In other poems the guacamayo, the brilliant red, yellow, and green macaw is equated with Atahualpa and the brilliant and socially advanced civilization of the Quechua people. In these poems Carrera does in words some of the things attempted by the Mexican muralists. They are the fruit of his long expatriation which has impelled him to search out and celebrate the values in the Ecuadorian heritage.

In the long poem, "Planetary Man," Carrera Andrade summarizes his themes, the isolation of the traveller, his delight in air, light, the bird, the insect, the planet. But man is the eternal despoiler, he exploits Juan Cordero and refuses him his due as a human being, with his creeping technology he dehumanizes social relations, he is everywhere the antithesis of creativity and the good life.

In this poem Carrera comes close to dealing with the newest catastrophe, the threat of pollution and the exhaustion of the earth as a planet able to support life. The poet is more directly concerned with moral sterility but it is moral sterility, a mindless materialism and acute indifference to any values except those of power and immediate gratification, which has led us to use science as a suicidal weapon. The poet manages a hopeful conclusion which is perhaps more temperamental than philosophical. We encounter a note of bitterness in several of his more recent poems. He expresses the sense of crisis that all sensitive men of our time must feel.

> In mouths there is only smoke,
> In eyes only distances.
> There is a drum in each ear.
> The Sahara yawns in the mind.

Even more bleak is the poem "The Terrestrians":

> They sell everything, even moonlight.
> They proclaim a worldwide cutting of Swan's throats
> To provide the basic material of a new industry.

Yet Carrera Andrade is too vital a person to abandon hope for the world which has nurtured him for more than half a century. Perhaps his most characteristic expression of faith, a sensuous faith which goes back to his very early landscapes of delight, is the poem "Weapons of Light" in which light is made the image of creativity and the humming-bird's death becomes a message of pantheism:

> But the heritage of the departed bird
> Is divided by insects and roots
> And the color of the wings goes to the
> Fruits, sweet planets,
> And from thence returns once more in golden pulp,
> In blood of plants...

What unifies all the themes of Carrera Andrade's work, visual sketches, social protest, preoccupation with objects, the delight in the universe, embodied in a rabbit or a rose, is the verbal texture. His is a poetry which does not abandon traditional literary elegance. While he does not shrink from simple everyday experience such as a horse stepping into the water at night:

The horse lifts its iron hoof
And plunges it into the water of dreams
With the slow movements of the dance.

or the falling of rain:

Rain, gliding with your transparent body,
Let fall your successive tunics
And stretch out on the ground like a crystal virgin.

or the vegetables in "les Halles":

The wine of twilight, ruddy in the beets,
Alarms the innocense of the lettuce.

this verbal elegance arises from a manner of perceiving and feeling which reserves for poetry a greater exaltation than that found in prose. Carrera is a classicist in that his language preserves a basic quality of Latin style which relates to tradition in Spanish, French, and Italian. He does not need to look for poetic subjects, all of life turns to poetry at his Midas touch.

In what way does Carrera Andrade's work reflect the specific New World experience? As has been pointed out above, he shares with North American poets a preoccupation with objects, with conceptualizing sensual experience. The Americas have never been noted for abstract philosophy. Faced with continents which had to be contained, which challenged man by their emptiness and which, up to now, he has tried violently to reshape in his own image, the American man of action has automatically become involved with things. The reflective American has been aware of this titanic rape, as yet only begun in the southern areas. His reaction has been to stress the need to perceive and absorb rather than deform and destroy. The European has, from time immemorial, known who he was and arrogantly assumed that everyone else accepts his own definition of himself. The

American is still defining himself in terms of his world and to do this he must observe his own world with the innocence of the newborn.

Finally, without centuries of static and smug conservatism behind him, the American poet is especially sensitive to the moral problems of his culture. Nowhere else in the world has literature been so steadily critical, so full of concern for the failure of the vision, so aware that the romantic utopia, the bright and beautiful dream, has been sullied by grasping acquisitiveness and stupidity.

Carrera Andrade is therefore truly a poet of the Americas, one who has been profoundly involved with the image of his own country and worked to shape it, one who with unfailing honesty has presented reality as he sees it, one who has never shirked the role he shares with his fellow artists, that of being the conscience of society.

LA GUIRNALDA DEL SILENCIO
1926

VIDA DE LA ALACENA

La alacena envejece roída de polilla
en la tibia hermandad de los muebles amigos.
Está ya deslustrada, y por instantes cruje
cual si fuera a morir. Si en la ronda los niños
hacen ruido la pobre sufre como una abuela
que ansía dormitar en su silencio tibio.
Ha olvidado el olor de las frutas maduras
y de aquel jugo de uvas de todos los domingos,
y, así tan viejecita como está, recuerda algo
sólo cuando el canario de la casa esta lírico.
Sus puertas han dañado los pequeños rateros
en busca de manzanas, en las noches de estío,
y la pobre alacena está ahora vacía...
Pero cuando la lámpara abre su ojo amarillo
se deja estar immóvil y muda, como en éxtasis
tal vez con el recuerdo de cuando éramos niños
mi prima y yo, abismados en un libro de estampas
sentados a la vieja y alta mesa de pino,
o de esa madrugada en que voló su alma
a la estrella que miran los amantes perdidos!

LIFE OF THE CUPBOARD

The cupboard grows old, gnawed by moths,
In the lukewarm sisterhood of friendly furniture.
She is dulled by time and now and then creaks
As if about to die. If the children are noisy
At their round games, the poor thing suffers like a grand-
    mother
Who wants to doze alone in her tepid silence.
She has forgotten the odor of ripe fruit
And of that grapejuice every Sunday
And, little old thing that she is, remembers something
Only when the house canary grows lyrical.
Little thieves in search of apples
On summer nights have damaged her doors
And now the poor cupboard is empty...
But when the lamp opens its yellow eye
She stops being motionless and mute as if pherhaps
She remembers in ecstacy the image of two children,
My cousin and I absorbed in a picture book,
Seated at the tall old pine table,
Or that sunrise in which her soul
Took flight to the star upon which lost lovers gaze.

3

MAL HUMOR

Chimeneas de sombreros alados,
torcidas chimeneas, paréntesis de campo
en la ciudad, gargantas
por donde sube triste la canción de las cosas:
— la canción familiar de la marmita,
del grillo y el fogón en la oscura cocina,
la canción de la silla de ruedas
y hasta el rumor monjil que hacen las puertas.

¡Chimeneas hostiles como armas
del odio de la urbe contra el azul que canta!
¡Humo sobre los techos: silenciosos disparos
contra el vuelo celeste de los pájaros!

¡Bah! Subid hasta el cielo, apuntad los gorriones,
dejad la tierra oscura de los hombres...
Mi alma también es una chimenea
en que arde la canción de las vidas pequeñas,
chimenea de hollín
que escupe, día, a día, un humo triste y denso
sobre el blanco papel del tomo inédito.

Chimneys with broad-brimmed hats,
Twisted chimneys, parentheses of country
In the city, throats
From which the sad song of objects rises:
The familiar song of the pot,
Of the cricket, and the stove in the dark kitchen,
The song of the wheelchair,
Even the nunlike murmur that doors make.

Chimneys, hostile as weapons
Of the city's anger against the singing blue!
Smoke above the roofs, silent discharge
Against the celestial flight of the birds.

Bah! Rise to the sky, aim at the sparrows,
Leave the dark land of men...
My soul, too, is a chimney
In which small lives burn,
A sooty chimney
Which, day after day spits out a thick, sad smoke
Upon the white paper of an unpublished book.

ISOLINA

Envuelta en una limpia claridad de manzana
va la tía Isolina con su paso monjil
lavando el comedor. Es su mano liviana
al sacudir el agua, un hisopo de abril.

Isolina es más blanca que la candeal harina,
más inocente y simple que el nevado mantel
cuando, desde la sombra rosa de la cocina,
hace sonar el tierno corazón del pastel.

Vara santa, florida de castas intenciones,
emplea su piedad desde que sale el sol
en fabricar compotas, en airear los melones
y en echar una perla de llanto en el perol.

Isolina: un revuelo de ropa almidonada
que aletea turbando el corredor monjil,
un olor de melones y una mano nevada
que nos roza las sienes en la luna de abril.

Wrapped in a limpid clarity of apple
Aunt Isolina moves with her nun's steps
As she washes the diningroom. Her light hand
Shaking out water is an April asperging.

Isolina is whiter than gleaming flour,
Simpler and more innocent than the snowy tablecloth
When, from the rosy darkness of the kitchen
She makes the tender heart of the pie ring out.

Sacred rod*, blossoming with chaste intentions.
Until sunrise her piety is busy with
Making compotes, with airing the melons
And dropping a pearl of tears into the copper pot.

Isolina: a flutter of starched skirts
That whips about disturbing the monastic corridor.
A fragrance of melons and a snowy hand
That strokes our temples in the April moonlight.

---

* Vara, a rod, tipped with felt, used for dusting churches.

EL RELOJ
A Jaime Torres Bodet

Reloj:
picapedrero del tiempo.

Golpea en la muralla más dura de la noche,
pica tenaz, el péndulo.

La despierta vainilla
compone partituras de olor en los roperos.

Vigilando el trabajo del reloj
anda con sus pantuflas calladas el silencio.

THE CLOCK

For Jaime Torres Bodet

Clock:
Stonecutter of time.

It strikes the hardest wall of night.
Obdurate chisel, the pendulum.

The vanilla awakens,
And composes partitas of fragrance in the clothes closets.

Overseeing the work of the clock,
Silence goes about in its hushed slippers.

LA CAMPANADA DE LA UNA

Desde la oscura torre que es un mástil de barco
la campanada de la una
baja en la noche como el cuerpo de un ahogado.

En la negra pizarra escribe su palote
la campanada de la una.
Casas de ojos vidriosos bucean en la noche.

El rabo entre las piernas, los vagabundos perros
a la campanada de la una
le ladran como a un muerto.

THE ONE O'CLOCK BELLNOTE

From the dark tower which is the mast of a ship
The one o'clock bellnote
Drops into the night like the body of a drowned man.

On the black slate the one o'clock bellnote
Writes a downstroke.
Houses with glassy eyes dive into the night.

Tails between their legs,
At the one o'clock bellnote, stray dogs
Bark as if at a dead man.

PRIMAVERA & COMPAÑIA

El almendro se compra un vestido
para hacer la primera comunión. Los gorriones
anuncian en las puertas su verde mercancía.
La primavera ya ha vendido
todas sus ropas blancas, sus caretas de enero
y sólo se ocupa de llevar hoy día
soplos de propaganda por todos los rincones.

Juncos de vidrio. Frascos de perfume volcados.
Alfombras para que anden los niños de la escuela.
Canastillos. Bastones
de los cerezos. Guantes muy holgados
del pato del estanque. Garza: sombrilla que vuela!

Máquina de escribir de la brisa en los hojas,
oloroso inventario.
Acudid al escaparate de la noche:
Cruz de diamantes, linternitas rojas
y de piedras preciosas un rosario.

Marzo ha prendido luces en la hierba
y el viejo abeto nútil se ha puesto anteojos verdes.
Hará la primavera, después de algunos meses,
un pedido de tarros de frutas en conserva
uvas — glándulas de cristal dulce —
y hojas doradas para empacar la tristeza.

SPRING AND COMPANY

The almond tree buys a dress
To take its first communion. The sparrows
Announce their green merchandise in doorways.
Spring has already sold
All of its white goods, its January masks,
And today is only concerned with puffing
Propaganda into every corner.

Rushes made of glass. Overturned bottles of perfume.
Rugs for schoolchildren to walk on.
Little baskets. Batons
Of cherries. Oversize gloves on
The ducks in the pond. Stork: a flying parasol.

Typewriter of breeze in the leaves,
Fragrant inventory.
Turn to the showcase of the night:
Cross of diamonds, little red lanterns
And rosary of precious stones.

March has lit sparks in the grass
And the useless old spruce tree has put on green spectacles.
After several months spring will have ready
An order of jars of preserved fruit,
Grapes — glands of sweet crystal —
And gilded leaves in which to pack sadness.

ABRIL

Tiempo en que el corazón quiere saltar descalzo
y en que al árbol le salen senos como a una niña.
Nos asalta el deseo de escribir nuestras cosas
con pluma de golondrina.

Estos charcos apenas son copas de agua clara
que arruga un aletazo o un canuto de hierba
y es el aire de vidrio una marea azul
donde el lento barquito del insecto navega.

Chapotean a gusto las sandalias del agua.
Los mosquitos parece que ciernen el silencio
y los gorriones cogen en el pico la perla
del buen tiempo.

A time in which the heart would like to go leaping barefoot
And in which the tree grows breasts like a young girl,
A desire seizes us to write down our impressions
With a swallow's feather.

These pools are no more than cups of clear water
Wrinkled by wingstrokes or a grass stem
And it is through the glassy air, a blue flood,
That the slow little craft of an insect navigates.

Sandals of water paddle freely about.
Silence appear to blossom with mosquitos
And the sparrows carry in their beaks
The pearl of fine weather.

MESETA

Caminos hacia el cielo. Letanías polares
lee el viento de noche en el libro del páramo.
Se siente el paternal vaho de la torada
y la bocina grita hacia el cielo estrellado,
mientras en las haciendas alumbran como lunas
los círculos de leche en los oscuros cántaros.
La madrugada sale como un alma de monja
a rondar los caminos. Y dá el cielo cristiano
al campo que madruga desayuno de estrellas.

¡Infantil alegría la que tienen los sacos!
Traviesos como niños que faltan a la escuela,
se estrechan fuertemente sobre el lomo del asno.
Asnillo: Te hartarás de briznas con luceros,
desde la puerta oirás la misa del poblacho,
y volverás de nuevo al diario trabajar
con una humilde y santa humedad en los párpados.

¿Ha hecho su vivienda el duende en el granero?
Sale por las rendijas un humo sonrosado.
Sentados sobre el trigo al roncar de una lámpara,
los señores del suelo se pasan conspirando:
abrazan a sus hombres, limpian las escopetas,
y todos se santiguan al chillido de un pájaro.

Dormitorio de hacienda, donde espanta a los sueños
Un moscardón que mueve el telar de su canto.
Las mesas espiritistas arañan la madera
y unos pasos sin cuerpo se escapan del armario
a la hora en que se filtra el hielo de la luna
y caen de las tapias las sombras de los campos
golpeadas por el sordo guijarro de un aullido.

Roads to the sky. Polar litanies
The night wind reads from the book of the paramo*.
Patriarchal steam from the cattle fills the air
And the horn of the herder shouts at the starry sky.
While in the haciendas disks of milk
Gleam like moons in dark earthen jars,
The dawn sallies forth like the soul of a nun
To roam the highways. And the christian heaven
Serves a breakfast of stars to the early rising fields.

What a childlike joy fills the sacks!
Mischievous as children playing hookey from school
They stretch out furtively across the donkey's back.
Little donkey: you stuff yourself with shoots of morning stars,
At the doorway you attend mass in the little hamlet
And turn once more to your everyday labor
With a saintly and humble moisture in your eyes.

Has the little elf made his home in the granary?
A rosy vapor issues from its crevices.
Seated on the wheat in the snoring lamplight
The masters of the soil pass the time conspiring,
Embrace their men, clean out their shotguns
And all cross themselves at the sharp cream of a bird.

Bedroom of the hacienda where a horsefly
Drives away dreams as he works at the web of his song.
Tipping tables that scratch their wood —
And bodiless footsteps escape from the cupboard
At the hour when the moon's ice filters in
And the shadows of the fields fall from mud walls
Struck by the muffled pebble of a howl.

---

* High mountain plain.

Letanías de muerte dice el viento del páramo.
Hace temblar de miedo la piel de la torada
y las lunas de leche en los oscuros cántaros.
Y mientras castamente la madrugada sale
como un alma de monja a rondar por el páramo,
suena como un lamento de la tierra baldía
la bocina que grita hacia el cielo estrellado.

The wind from the paramo recites litanies of death
Makes the hides of the cattle
And the moons of milk tremble with fear on the dark earthen
jars.
And while the morning chastely sallies forth
Like the soul of a nun to roam the páramo,
The horn that shouts at the starry sky
Sounds like a lament from the wild, untilled earth.

CANCION BREVE DEL ESPANTAJO

El espantajo
un tráfico de brisas
ordena en los sembrados.

Cuida en el buen sol
la uva picada,
barril del gorrión.

En el circo del campo
danza y gesticula
vegetal payaso.

Un ladrido azul
le dá el horizonte:
mordiscos de luz.

Le invitan caminos
y le burlan pájaros
a vuelos y a silbos.

Y le dá el ocaso
una cruz de sombra
al espantajo.

BRIEF SONG OF THE SCARECROW

The scarecrow,
A traffic of breezes,
Creates order in the tilled fields.

In the good sunlight
He tends the bird-pecked grape
Watercask of sparrows.

In the circus of the fields
He dances and gesticulates.
Vegetable clown.

The horizon
Barks at him with blue:
Bites of light.

The roads invite him.
Birds mock him
With flutterings and whistles.

And sunset bestows
A cross of shadow
Upon the scarecrow.

BOLETINES DE MAR Y TIERRA

1928 - 1930

BOLETIN DE VIAJE

Sobre el tejado del mundo
puso el gallo a secar su canto de colores.
La luz era pesada como un fruto.

Sus tablas de la ley me entregó el campo.
De la antigua madera de la cruz
estaba hecho el arado.

Era un anillo de dolor
la línea ecuatorial
en el dedo del corazón.

En la nave de veinte cornetas
embarqué mi baúl de papagayos
hacia otro extremo de la tierra.

Ardía el alfabeto de las constelaciones.
Giraban gozosos los puertos niños
en el carrusel del horizonte.

Se amotinaron los mares
y los cuatro vientos
contra mi sueño almirante.

Ancla: Trébol de hierro.
Te arrojó el Capitán al continente antiguo.
Ví las torres cargadas con sus sacos de nubes
y las grúas cigüeñas
con su cesta en el pico.

Europa hacía andar con un ritmo de aceite
los arados mecánicos.
Con su pajita tornasol
la espiga chupaba el calcio.

Over the tiled roof of the world
The cock hung out his bright colored chant to dry.
The light was by then as heavy as a fruit.

The country offered me tablets of the law.
The plow was made of the ancient wood
of the cross.

The latitude of the equator was
A ring of pain
On the finger of the heart.

In a ship with twenty funnels
I launched my baggage of parrots
Toward the other end of the world.

The alphabet of the constellations blazed.
Like children the ports whirled gayly
On the carousel of the horizon.

The seas and the four winds
Mutinied
Against my admiral dreams.

Anchor: iron cloverleaf.
The captain plucked you from an ancient continent
I saw the towers laden with their sacks of clouds
And the derricks, storks
With baskets in their beaks.

Europe set mechanical plows
Going with a rythm of oil.
Through its irridescent straw
The wheat sucked at the lime of the soil.

Mas, toda la alegría del mundo
al subir por las chimeneas
se convertía en humo.

En la hoja en blanco de la harina
imprimían los molinos
la arenga proletaria de la espiga.

Las ciudades se hablaban a lo largo del aire.
Descubrí al hombre. Entonces
comprendí mi mensaje.

But all the joy of the world
As it rose through chimneys
Was converted into smoke.

On the blank page of flour
Mills were printing
The wheat's proletarian oratory.

Cities were speaking through the breadth of the air.
I discovered man. Then
I understood my message.

COSTAS DEL DIA

El pensamiento de los golfos
lo comentaban las velas.
Se habían comido los peces
la luna, gorra marinera.

Con sus alforzas de vidrio
giraba el mar redondo.
Al són de un viento de vitela
cantaban los mástiles sordos.

Llegaban luces nadadoras
desde las costas del día.
Con sus agujas de sal
el aire en el puente cosía.

Dormían las islas ángeles
a las orillas del cielo.
En la canoa de una nube
remaba el sol marinero.

The sails were commenting
On the sinking of the gulfs.
The fish had eaten
The moon, a seaman's cap.

The round sea whirled
Its glassy braids.
The deaf masts were singing
To the music of a parchment wind.

Lights were arriving, swimmers
From the coast of day,
With its salt needles
The air was sewing up the bridge.

The angel islands were sleeping
On the shores of the sky.
The seagoing sun paddled off
In the canoe of a cloud.

EL DESAYUNO DEL MUNDO

Las cuatro horas — desnudas niñas
parten en cuatro tajadas
la mañana de sandía.

Un ojo azul se abre en la altura.
Aprenden los niños del mundo
el Catecismo del azúcar.

Del teatro de terciopelo de la noche
salen las ventanas
con los ojos bañados en lágrimas.

Los relojes no cesan de cantar
su canto de polilla
en un huequito de la eternidad.

Van haciéndose agua
en el cielo de sandía
las estrellas azucaradas.

Toma el mundo recién lavado
sus cucharadas de luz
con rebanadas de campo.

THE WORLD'S BREAKFAST

Four o'clock, four naked girls
Divide the watermelon of morning
Into four portions.

A blue eye opens at the zenith.
The children of the world learn
The catechism of sugar.

From the velvet theatre of night
The windows emerge,
Their eyes bathed in tears.

Clocks do not cease to sing
Their mothlike song
In the little hollow of eternity.

The sugar-sprinkled stars
Go turning to water
Through the watermelon sky.

The newly washed world
Takes its spoonfuls of light
With slices of meadow.

PUERTO A LAS OCHO

En los barriles duerme un sueño de ginebra.
Los barriles de noche tienen el vino triste
y añoran el descanso tibio de la bodega.

Huele el aire del muelle como un cesto de ostiones
y es una red oscura, puesta a secar, la noche.

Los mástiles son cañas para pescar estrellas
y estas barcazas sólo son canastas de pesca.

La lámpara de a bordo
salta como un gran pez
chorreando sobre el puente su fulgor escamoso.

Pequeñas lucecitas navegan en la noche,
como si un contrabando de muertos
llevaran sobre el agua los siniestros lanchones.

PORT AT EIGHT O'CLOCK

In the casks a dream of gin lies asleep.
The casks of night hold a sad wine
And long for the tepid repose of the wine-vault.

The air of the quai smells like a tray of oysters
And the night is a dark net put out to dry.

The masts are poles to fish for stars
And the barges are baskets of fish.

The lamp on board
Jumps like a great fish,
Dripping its scaly radiance over the bridge.

Tiny lights navigate in the night
As if a crew of smuggled dead men
Were guiding small lighters over the water.

GUAYAQUIL

Hablan del sol los portales,
las canoas de la ría
y el Astillero sin nadie.

Tan sólo una sombra blanca
su pregón lanza en el viento.
La luz pinta las persianas.

LA HABANA

La Habana cuenta sus frutas
y planta sus chimeneas,
inmensas cañas de azúcar.

Emigran los cocoteros.
Se van el ron y la rumba
y crecen los rascacielos.

NUEVA YORK DE NOCHE

Nueva York muestra en la sombra
sus escaleras al cielo
y sus ríos con antorchas.

Sus ventanas son crisoles
donde se convierte en luz
la esperanza de los hombres.

GUAYAQUIL

The vestibules,
The canoes in the estuary
And the empty shipyard speak of sun.

Only a white shadow
Releases its street cry in the wind.
Light paints the windowblinds.

HAVANA

Havana counts its fruit
And plants its chimneys,
Immense sugar canes.

The cocopalms emigrate.
Rum and rhumba depart
And the skyscrapers flourish.

NEW YORK AT NIGHT

In the darkness New York displays
Its stairways to the sky
And its rivers with their torches.

Its windows are crucibles
Where men's hopes
Are converted into light.

CUADERNO DE POEMAS INDIOS
1928

DOMINGO

Iglesia frutera
sentada en una esquina de la vida:
Naranjas de cristal de las ventanas.
Organo de cañas de azúcar.

Angeles: polluelos
de la Madre María.

La campanilla de ojos azules
sale con los pies descalzos
a corretear por el campo.

Reloj de Sol.
Burro angelical con su sexo inocente;
Viento buenmozo del domingo
que trae noticias del cerro.

Indias con su carga de legumbres
abrazada a la frente.

El cielo pone los ojos en blanco
cuando sale corriendo de la iglesia
la campanilla de los pies descalzos.

Fruitseller church
Seated at the corner of life:
Windows crystal oranges,
The organ canes of sugar.

Angels: Mother Mary's
Little chickens.

The bell with blue eyes
Goes off on bare feet
To wander about the country.

Sun clock:
Angelic burro with its innocent sex;
Wind, in his Sunday best,
Bringing news of the mountains.

Indian women with their load of vegetables
Embracing their foreheads.

The sky rolls up its eyes
When it sees the churchbell
Come running out of the church barefoot.

SIERRA

Ahorcadas en la viga del techo
con sus alas de canario las mazorcas.

Conejillos de Indias
engañan al silencio analfabeto
con chillidos de pájaro y arrullos de paloma.

Hay en la choza una muda carrera
cuando el viento empuja la puerta.

La montaña brava
ha abierto su oscuro paraguas de nubes
con varillas de rayos.

El Francisco, el Martín, el Juan:
Trabajando en la hacienda del cerro
les habrá sorprendido el temporal.

Un aguacero de pájaros
cae chillando en los sembrados.

Ears of corn gibbeted from the roofpoles
With their canarybird wings.

Guinea pigs
Deceive the illiterate silence
With bird squeaks and the cooing of doves.

There is a mute action in the hut
When the wind pushes the door.

The rough mountain
Has opened its dark umbrellas of cloud
With ribs of lightning.

Our Francisco, our Martín, our Juan:
Working in the mountain hacienda,
The thunder shower will have caught them.

A downpour of birds
Falls shrieking into the tilled fields.

FIESTA DE SAN PEDRO

Alazán, Alazán.
Después de la cena ciruela
a carrera tendida hacía el pueblo
de sombreros de paja del páramo.

El montado lleva en el ala del poncho
un rollo de viento.

Carteles estremecidos de grítos
en los estancos del camino.

Redobla en las orejas el viento tambor.
Corren en fila india los árboles del cerro.

Echa su lazo de hielo un aullido
a la garganta del silencio.

Con su peineta de luminarias
la primera casa del pueblo.

Han venido los peones de Santa Prisca
con sus ponchos color de ciruela:
borrachos de fuegos artificiales
se arriman al hombro de las puertas.

La Rueda chillona! La Rueda de luces! La Rueda!

Muere acribillada de cohetes
la noche de ojos de aguardiente.

FIESTA OF SAN PEDRO

Sorrel-colored horse, sorrel-colored horse.
After the meal of cherries,
A rush toward the village,
Roofed with straw hats from the paramos.

The horseman carries a roll of wind
In the wing of his poncho.

Billboards on the liquor-shops by the road
Shaken by shouts.

The drum of the wind echoes in our ears.
The mountain trees are running in Indian file.

A howl throws its lasso of ice
Around the throat of silence.

With its hairdo of lights,
The first house of the village.

The peons of Santa Prisca have come
With their cherry-colored ponchos,
Drunk on fireworks
They lean on the shoulders of doorways.

The screaming Wheel! The lighted Wheel! The Wheel!

Night, with brandy eyes,
Dies pierced by rockets.

INDIADA

La garúa del monte
hace chillar las últimas candelas
rotas en resplandores.

Los comuneros llevan la mañana
enredada en los dientes de sus hoces
hacia la tierra baja.

En el vaho de los ponchos serranos
colorados como manzanas
aletean las voces y los pájaros.

Hacia la tierra gorda de gavillas,
en el ala cóncava de los sombreros
baja el viento del páramo.

Los caminos arrieros conducen en la noche
en los carros del aire
racimos de canciones.

La indiada lleva la mañana
en la protesta de sus palas.

INDIAN CROW

In the drizzle of the mountain
The last candles hiss,
Refracted into brilliancy.

Toward the lowlands
The Indians of the commune carry the morning
Caught in the teeth of their sickles.

In the vapor from mountain ponchos,
The color of apples,
Flutter voices and birds.

Toward the earth, fat with sheaves,
The wind from the páramo
Descends in the concave brim of their hats.

Muleteer roads drive bunches of song
Through the night
In carts of air.

The Indian crowd carries the morning
In the protest of its shovels.

LEVANTAMIENTO

1.

Iban delante nuestros padres
buscando el vado de la tarde crecida
con sus pies cargados de memoria.

Ochocientas voluntades. Ochocientas.
Para el ancho redoble de nuestras sandalias
era un tambor la tierra.

Tierra vestida a cuadros,
mordida por los cercos guardianes:
Estas prisionera de cuatro hombres
hasta el último azul del horizonte.

Traíamos el pulso de la semilla libre,
tierra de pechos vegetales.
Flameaba el harapo de nuestro grito
en el palo más alto del aire.

Con su carrera de sangre los soldados
despertaron los verdes quietos del campo.

Avanzaban comidos de sombra,
y un estribillo de dientes afilados
mordía sus hebillas luminosas.

Con los tallos negros de sus fusiles
les vieron pasar
los ojos franciscanos de las sementeras.

Nosotros camínábamos escoltados de espigas,
con un poncho de luz sobre los hombros
y en la frente el mandato de la tierra.

1.

Our fathers went before us,
Seeking the pathway of growing twilight,
Their feet laden with memory.

Eight hundred wills. Eight hundred.
The earth was a drum
For the resounding echo of our sandals.

Land dressed in parcels
Bitten by guardian fences,
You are prisoner of four men
As far as the final blue of the horizon.

We bore in us the pulse of free seed,
Land of vegetable breasts.
The rag of our cries fluttered
From the tallest pole of the air.

With their bloody action the soldiers
Awoke the quiet green of the fields.

They advanced eaten by shadow
And a refrain of sharp teeth
Gnawed their glittering buckles.

The Franciscan eyes of the fields
Saw them pass
With the black stalks of their guns.

We went forward escorted by wheat ears.
With a poncho of light over our shoulders
And on our foreheads the mandate of the earth.

2.

Soldados, Soldados.
Ejercicios de puntería
sobre los colores humildes del campo.

Vagabunda muralla de humo:
trampa abierta en el día.
Nos matan desde el horizonte
dando a luz estrellas lívidas.

Compañeros:
los fusiles nos miran con sus ojos de muerto.

Golpea el mundo en nuestras sienes.
El miedo de morir grita en nuestra garganta.

Hay que salvar a la carrera
el silencio listado de mortales bengalas.

Ochocientos bajamos de los cerros,
contando nuestros padres, nuestras madres
y nuestros tíernos hijos.
               A esta hora
casi todos descansan sobre la tierra grande.

Traíamos el pulso de la semilla libre,
tierra acorralada por los cercos guardianes.
A la orilla del viento acampó la canción.
El fusíl desplomó nuestro mensaje.

Tumbados en la vecindad del cielo
nuestros muertos duermen
manando un cosmos dulce del costado
y con una corona de sudor en la frente.

2.

Soldiers, Soldiers.
Target practice
Against the humble colors of the countryside.

Drifting walls of smoke:
Pitfall opened in the day.
They killed us from the horizon,
Giving birth to livid stars.

Comrades:
The guns are looking at us with eyes of death.

The world beats in our temples.
The fear of death shouts in our throats.

We must rush onward through silence
Striped with deadly Bengal fires.

Eight hundred we came down from the mountains,
Counting our fathers, our mothers
And our gentle children
                              And now
Nearly all are resting on the broad earth.

We bore the seed, the pulse of freedom,
The earth hemmed in by guardian fences.
The song was encamped on the shores of the wind.
The gun shattered our message.

Buried in the neighborhood of the sky,
Our dead sleep,
A sweet cosmos flowing from their sides
And a crown of sweat on their foreheads.

EL TIEMPO MANUAL

1935

SOLEDAD DE LAS CIUDADES

Sin conocer mi número.
Cercado de murallas y de límites.
Con una luna de forzado,
y atada a mi tobillo una sombra perpetua.

Fronteras vivas se levantan
a un paso de mis pasos.

No hay norte ni sur, este ni oeste,
sólo existe la soledad multiplicada,
la soledad dividida por una cifra de hombres.
La carrera del tiempo en el circo del reloj,
el ombligo luminoso de los tranvías,
las campanas de hombros atléticos
los muros que deletrean dos o tres palabras de color,
están hechos de una materia solitaria.

Imagen de la soledad:
El albañil que canta en un andamio,
fija balsa del cielo.
Imagenes de la soledad:
El viajero que se sumerge en un periódico.
El camarero que esconde un retrato en el pecho.

La ciudad tiene apariencia mineral.
La geometría urbana es menos bella
que la que aprendimos en la escuela.
Un triángulo, un huevo, un cubo de azúcar
nos iniciaron en la fiesta de las formas.
Sólo después fué la circunferencia:
la primera mujer y la primera luna.

SOLITUDE OF CITIES

Without knowing my number,
Fenced by walls and boundaries,
With a moon sentenced to hard labor
And a perpetual shadow tied to my heels.

Living frontiers arise
One step from my steps.

There is no north, south, east or west,
Nothing but multiplied solitude exists,
Solitude divided by a quantity of men,
The course of time in the circle of the watch,
The luminous navel of stretcars,
Bells with athletic shoulders:
The walls which spell out two or three colored words
Are made of solitary stuff.

Image of solitude:
The mason singing on a scaffold,
Raft anchored in sky.
Images of solitude:
The passenger buried in a newspaper,
The waiter who hides a picture in his vest pocket.

In the city of stone
Urban geography is less beautiful
Than the kind we learned at school.
A triangle, an egg, a cube of sugar
Initiated us into the festivity of shapes.
After that there was only circumference:
The first woman and the first moon.

¿Dónde estuviste soledad,
que no te conocí hasta los veinte años?
En los trenes, los espejos y las fotografías
siempre estás a mi lado.

Los campesinos están menos solos
porque forman una misma cosa con la tierra.
Los árboles son hijos suyos,
los cambios de tiempo observan en su propia carne
y les sirve de ejemplo la santoral de los animalitos.

Esta soledad es nutrida de libros,
de paseos, de pianos y pedazos de muchedumbre,
de ciudades y cielos conquistados por la máquina,
de pliegos de espuma
desenrollándose hasta el límite del mar.
Todo se ha inventado.
Mas no hay nada que pueda librarnos de la soledad.

Los naipes guardan el secreto de los desvanes.
Los sollozos están hechos para ser fumados en pipa.
Se ha tratado de enterrar la soledad en una guitarra.
Se sabe que anda por los pisos desalquilados,
que comercia con los trajes de los suicidas
y que enreda los mensajes en los hilos telegráficos.

Where were you solitude
That I never knew you until I was twenty?
In trains, in mirrors and in photographs,
You are always by my side.

Countryfolk are less alone
Because they are the same thing as the earth.
The trees are their sons,
They sense the change of the season in their own flesh;
And the lives of saintly little animals are an example to them.

This solitude is nourished by books,
By boulevards, by pianos and fragments of multitude,
By cities and skies conquered by the machine.
By folds of foam
Unrolling to the ultimate boundaries of the sea.
We have invented everything
But nothing can free us from solitude.

Playing cards keep the secret of attics.
Sobs are made to be smoked in a pipe.
Attempts have been made to bury solitude in a guitar.
We know that it walks through vacant apartments,
That it has business with the clothes of suicides,
And that it entangles messages in telegraph wires.

COLOR DE LA HABANA

Sonando el tambor de sus hojas una tribu de cocoteros
    salvajes.
Mar en continuo parpadeo de fosforescencias.
La Habana sale todos los días a los muelles
a esperar la llegada de los barcos.
mientras sus nadadores sacan entre los dientes las monedas
que van a saludar a los peces en el mar antillano.
Sus tranvías aprenden el compás de las maracas,
sus arbolitos se alinean como borregos
y sus avenidas corren hasta encontrar una estatua.

Mujeres de piel de tabaco caliente y de canela.
Criollos con su sombrero de paja que el trópico madura.
Negritos cuya risa se abre como una sandía.
Cocos y guanábanas, despojos de la rumba.

En la Avenida de los Presidentes se multiplican los hongos
y los cañones del Parque Maceo bostezan de hambre
viendo saltar los peces en la bahía
cuya entrada prohibe con su dedo en alto el Castillo del
    Morro.

Doscientos guardias se cuadran cada día
ante la mirada azul del diamante del Capitolio.
Letreros y ventanas dictan un curso práctico de inglés
en los cuadernos cuadriculados de los rascacielos.
Mas las flores son caras en la Avenida Veintitrés
y la luz tiene el color del maní y el aceite de girasol.

En la Avenida Ocho se ha encontrado una piña de fuego
madurando sus semillas de muerte junto a la casa del Fiscal.

THE COLOR OF HAVANA

A tribe of savage cocopalms beating its drums of leaves.
Sea a continual blinking of phosforescences.
Every day Havana comes down to the quais
To wait for the ships to come in
While its swimmers retrieve between their teeth
Coins which sink to greet the antillean fish.
Its streetcars learn the music of maraccas.
Its little trees line up like lambs
And its avenues run to meet a statue.

Women with skins of warm tobacco and cinnamon
Creoles with straw hats ripened in the tropics.
Little Negroes whose laughter opens like a watermelon.
Cocopalms and custard apples, spoils of the rhumba.

On the Avenue of the Presidents mushrooms multiply
And the cannons of Maceo Park yawn with hunger,
Seeing fish jump in the bay
Whose entrance is prohibited by the raised finger of Morro
    Castle.

Two hundred guards are drawn up each day
Before the blue diamond stare of the Capitol.
Signs and shop windows dictate a practical course in English
In the cubed notebooks of skyscrapers.
But flowers are expensive on Twenty Third Avenue
And the light is the color of peanut and sunflowerseed oil.

On Eighth Avenue a pinecone of fire was found
Ripening its seeds of death next to the Mansion of Justice.

Sin embargo, el aire destapa sus mariscos vivificantes en
    el malecón
y la vida se azucara en los jardines de la Tropical.

Nada pasa aquí sino una cadera de música
y unos brazos de fruta que hacen equivocarse a los pájaros.
Un aeroplano vestido de blanco va recortando el calor
con su ventilador ambulante.

Los barquichuelos dan su lección de sueño frente a La
    Cabaña
y los fleteros negros exhalan sus cantos de humo
hacia el horizonte donde empieza a piar el primer lucero.
No sorprende a nadie el atentado terrorista del crepúsculo.
Y la luna menguante cuelga como un plátano
del bananero del cielo.

Nevertheless the air opens the shell of fresh seafood on the
    Maleçon*
And life is sprinkled with sugar in the gardens of La Tropical.
Here nothing happens except musical hips
And arms which the birds mistake for fruit.
An Airplane dressed in white passes stirring the heat
    with its moving fan.

Little boats give lessons in sleep in front of La Cabana
And the Negro porters exhale songs of smoke
Toward the horizon where the first evening star begins to
    chirp.
No one is surprised at the terrorist conspiracy of the twilight
And the waning moon hangs like a banana
From the plantain of the sky.

---

* Avenue which runs along the harbor.

EDICION DE LA TARDE

La tarde lanza su primera edición de golondrinas
anunciando la nueva política del tiempo,
la escasez de las espigas de la luz,
los navíos que salen a flote en el astillero del cielo,
el almacén de sombras del poniente,
los motines y desórdenes del viento,
el cambio de domicilio de los pájaros,
la hora de apertura de los luceros.

La súbita defunción de las cosas
en la marea de la noche ahogadas,
los débiles gritos de auxilio de los astros
desde su prisión de infinito y de distancia,
la marcha incesante de los ejércitos del sueño
contra la insurrección de los fantasmas
y al filo de las bayonetas de la luz, el orden nuevo
implantado en el mundo por el alba.

The evening puts out its first edition of swallows
Announcing the new politics of the hour,
Scarcity of light's wheatears,
A fleet of ships sails from the shipyard of the sky,
The department store of shadows in the west,
The mutinies and disorders of the wind,
The birds moving to new addresses,
The time when the evening stars will appear.

The sudden death of things
Drowned in the tide of nightfall,
The weak cries for help from the stars
From their prison of distance and infinity,
The incessant marching of dream armies
Against the insurrection of ghosts,
And, at the points of light's row of bayonets,
The new order imposed upon the world by dawn.

SERVICIO

Las aguas del cielo, religiosas sirvientas de los árboles
lavan llorando las cortezas
y sirven cubos llenos a la sed de las ramas.
Nodrizas de los frutos niños,
los mecen con un canto de frescura
aprendido en su viaje vertical por la atmósfera.

Sólo los pájaros saben su aventura:
la ascención colectiva por rutas de calor,
el vuelo lento en el dirigible de una nube,
la maniobra aérea de las falanges transparentes
y su vuelta a la tierra en claras muchedumbres.

Ya repartidos por igual todos sus cántaros,
las aguas desanudan sus anzuelos frescos
y van a pescar burbujas en las charcas,
esas provincias líquidas del cielo.

SERVICE

Waters from the sky, pious servants of the trees,
Weep as they wash their bark
And serve brimming buckets to the thirst of branches.
Wetnurses to infant fruit
They rock them to a song of coolness,
Learned on their vertical voyage through the atmosphere.

Only the birds know this adventure;
The collective ascension by pathways of warmth
The slow flight in the dirigible of a cloud.
The aerial maneuver of transparent phalanxes
And their return to earth in sparkling multitudes.

Now, with all their pitchers impartially emptied,
The waters disentangle their cool fishhooks,
And fish for bubbles in the pools,
Those liquid provinces of the sky.

POEMAS DE PASADO MAÑANA

I

Las piedras escalaron en hileras la altura
y se superpusieron el acero y el barro,
las maderas forzudas que soportan un muro en sus **hombros**
y los claros ladrillos que lanzan sones áureos.

El edificio se incorporó poco a poco
desnudando de andamios su pecho de cemento
con un soplo de vida en sus agujeros más recónditos
y sus chimeneas como pilares del cielo.

Las voces, las pisadas invadieron la fábrica
y dieron su jugo de fuerza los músculos maduros.
Iniciaron las máquinas su música industrial
que se escapó a las nubes por una escala de humo.

II

Las bielas movían sus ágiles codos
y las ruedas continuaban su volatín incesante
entre las palmadas de las fajas de cuero
y las risas sin fin de los motores unánimes.

La gimnasia monótona e infantil de las máquinas
se hacía cada vez con un ritmo más rápido,
hasta que gritaba el pito de la fábrica
como la sirena de un navío de forzados.

Las manufacturas viajaban por millares
hacia las ciudades más lejanas del Globo.
En su lugar volvía el oro en abundancia:
los carros y las pieles de los días más prósperos.

POEMS OF THE DAY AFTER TOMORROW

I

Rows of stones scaled the heights
Steel and cement rested upon them,
The stout beams that support a wall on their shoulders
And the bright tiles that emit golden sounds.

Little by little the building took form,
Its cement breast, stripped of scaffolding
With a breath of life in its most secret crevices
And its chimneys like pillars of the sky.

Voices, footsteps invaded the factory
And fullgrown muscles bestowed their liquid of power.
The machine begin their industrial music
That escaped to the clouds on a staircase of smoke.

II

The connecting rods moved their agile elbows
And wheels continued their incessant somersaults
Among the clapping of leather belts
And the endless laughter of synchronized motors.

The monotonous and childish gymnasium of the machines
Accelerated with an ever more rapid motion.
Until the factory whistle screamed
Like the siren of a shipful of convicts.

The goods made here traveled by thousands
Toward the most distant cities of the globe.
In their place an abundance of gold returned:
Cars and furs of the most prosperous times.

Cada alba soñaba edificios de vidrio.
Chimeneas y cúpulas brotaban de la tierra.
Mas, un día, los puertos del mundo se cerraron
y las manufacturas colmaron las bodegas.

Las bielas, los motores se pararon a un tiempo
en un vasto cementerio de máquinas.
Los brazos se cruzaron ante esa lenta muerte.
El cielo izó su bandera en la fábrica cerrada.

III

Juan, el de las manos que hacen girar las ruedas,
Pedro que norma el hondo pulso de los motores,
y otros cien compañeros
salieron de la fábrica con rumbo hacia los hombres.

El vacío bostezaba en los armarios
de la vivienda obrera,
y se agrupaba en torno de la mesa sin pan
el coro silencioso de las bocas abiertas.

Despojando la calle de sus luces
los huelguistas pasaban sin cesar hacia el norte
como un río de sombra
que se vierte en el ancho golfo del horizonte.

Pedro, Juan y los otros campañeros
se pusieron al ritmo de la marcha y el canto
y se unieron al bosque innumerable
que amenazaba ahogar la fábrica en sus brazos.

Every sunrise dreamed glass buildings.
Chimneys and cupolas sprouted from the earth,
But, one day the doors of the world shut
And piles of goods glutted the stores.

The rods and the motors stopped all at once
In a great cemetery of machines
Arms were folded, faced with this slow death.
And the sky raised its flag over the closed factory.

III

Juan, he with the hands who makes the wheels turn,
Pedro who regulates the deep pulse of the motors,
And a hundred other comrades
Went out of the factory in the direction of other men.

Emptiness yawned in the larders
Of the workers' houses
And the silent chorus of open mouths
Clustered around tables without bread.

Despoiling the street of its lights
The strikers continued to go north
Like a river of shadows
Which empties in the broad gulf of the horizon.

Pedro, Juan and the other comrades
Became part of the rythm of marching and song
And an innumerable forest came together
Threatening to strangle the factory in its arms.

IV

Camaradas: el mundo está construído sobre nuestros muertos
y nuestros pies han creado todas las rutas.
Mas, bajo el cielo de todos, no hay un palmo de sombra
para nosostros que hemos hecho florecer las cúpulas.

El pan, nieto rubio del sembrador, el techo
— fronda de barro y sol que cubre la familia —,
el derecho de amar y de andar, no son nuestros:
Somos los negreros de nuestra propia vida.

La dicha, el mar que no hemos visto nunca,
las ciudades que jamás visitaremos
se alzan en nuestros puños cerrados como frutos
anunciando la más grave cosecha de los tiempos.

¡Sólo el derecho a morir, camaradas del mundo!
Cien manos se reparten las ofrendas del Globo.
Tiempo es ya de lanzarse a las calles y plazas
a rescatar la Obra construída por nosotros.

V

Un paso más hacia la floresta de la pólvora
al Continente de los frutos de plomo,
donde los piés se enredan en invisibles zarzas.
Ciegos los ojos.

— Buen camarada, llévale este abrazo a mi madre...
Cae el obrero.
(A un mundo con viviendas baratas y jardines
        van los obreros muertos).

IV

Comrades: The world is constructed upon our dead
And our feet have created all the paths.
Moreover under every sky, there is not handsbreadth of
     shadow
For us, we who made the cupolas blossom.

Bread, blond grandchild of the sower, the roof —
Foliage of clay and sun which shelters the family —
The right to love and walk everywhere are not ours:
We are slavetraders in our own lives.

Happiness, the sea that we have never seen,
The cities that we shall never visit
We raise in our clenched fists like fruit,
Announcing the most serious harvest of all time.

Only the right to die, comrades of the world!
A hundred hands share the offerings of the earth.
It is time to hurl ourselves into the streets and squares
To redeem the Work that we ourselves constructed.

V

One step more toward the fair field of powder
Toward the Continent of leaden fruit.
Where the feet are trapped in invisible brambles,
Eyes going blind.

— Good comrade, bear this embrace to my mother...
The worker falls.
(Dead workers go to a world of cheap food and gardens).

Ametralladora, perro de la muerte:
tu ladrar cesa.
Unos hombres de blusa llegan cantando
de los cuatro extremos de la tierra.

Machinegun, dog of death:
Your barking ceases.
Many men in blouses arrive singing
From the four corners of the earth.

LA ALQUIMIA VITAL

Un viejo vive en mi fabricando mi muerte.
A su soplo se tornan en ceniza los años,
los frutos descomponen sus azúcares
y la escarcha visita mi laberinto orgánico.

Viento, agujas y pálidas sustancias
manipula este huésped emboscado.
A veces, mientras duermo, se escucha un dulce liquido
que se vierte en su cántaro.

Ha bañado mi piel con su amarilla química.
Ha moderado el clima de mi mano.
En lugar de mi rostro, el suyo con arrugas
en los espejos hallo.

Conspira en lo más hondo
donde la entraña tiembla — animal fatigado —
y entre verdes sustancias y retortas de hielo
fabricando mi muerte deja pasar los años.

THE ALCHEMY OF LIFE

An old man lives in me devising my death.
His breath turns the years to ashes,
While sweet fruits turn sour
And frost visits the labyrinth of my organs.

This guest in ambuscade manipulates
Wind, needles and pallid substances.
At times while I sleep a sweet liquid can be heard
Being poured into his pitcher.

He has bathed my skin with his yellow chemicals.
He has changed the climate of my hand.
Instead of my face, I discover
His own wrinkled one in mirrors.

He conspires in the depths of my being
Where my heart trembles like a tired animal
And among green substances and retorts full of ice
As the years go by he devises my death.

LUGAR DE ORIGEN
1945-1947

DIAS IMPARES

Hay días que amanecen muy temprano
con sus ojos de buey y su frente nublada,
sin recordar su nombre
acaso equivocados de semana.

Días en que no hallamos las calles y las fechas,
nos rehusa la luz su guía pura
olvidamos las rosas y los números,
las ventanas nos muestran sólo estampas adustas.

Extraviamos la llave del tesoro,
la consigna de amor convertida en anillo,
batallamos con cartas y memorias,
confundimos la sombra y un vestido.

Días de arena, que hacen sucumbir los relojes,
días en que bajamos peldaños de ceniza,
en que todos los muros de la casa nos niegan
y buscamos en vano la puerta de salida.

DISPLACED DAYS

There are days when dawn comes very early
With ox-eyes and a cloudy forehead, days
With unremembered names,
Perhaps a mistake made in the week.

Days on which we can not find streets or dates
And the light denies us its pure beacon,
We forget roses and numbers,
Windows reveal only sullen vistas.

The key to the treasure has gone astray,
Love's watchword converted into a ring,
We struggle with letters and memories,
We mistake the shadows for a dress.

Days of sand which immobilize clocks,
Days in which we descend steps of ashes
On which every wall in the house denies us
And we look in vain for the door to freedom.

TRIBUTO A LA NOCHE

Niegas, oh testaruda, lo que el día ha afirmado
y después de su muerte, de las cosas te adueñas
Tus sacos de carbón abarrotan sin término
la universal bodega.

Tu gran cuerpo de sombra en el mundo no cabe,
nebuloso animal nutrido de guitarras,
y distraes el tiempo de tu prisión terrestre
borrando los caminos y devorando lámparas.

Entras a todas partes, habitante del cielo
y te instalas sin ruido entre nosotros
o te quedas mirándonos detrás de las ventanas
con tus tiernos ojillos eternos y remotos.

Caminante puntual, nodriza de campanas,
vas metiendo en tu fardo los seres y las cosas.
Me ofreces tu enlutado palacio, y me reclino
en tu almohada de sombra.

TRIBUTE TO NIGHT

Obstinate night, you deny what the day has affirmed
And, after its death, make yourself master of everything.
Your bags of coal continually
Overstock the universal warehouse.

Cloudy animal, nourished on guitars,
Your great body of shadow doesn't fit into the world
And you while away the time in your earthly prison
Blotting out roads and devouring lamps.

Heavenly citizen, you enter everywhere
And soundlessly take your place among us
Or you are content to look at us through windows
With your tender little eyes, both remote and timeless.

Punctual wanderer, wetnurse of churchbells,
You pass, filling your bundle with people and things.
You offer me your crepe-shrouded palace
And I recline on your pillow of darkness.

AQUI YACE LA ESPUMA

La espuma, dulce monja, en su hospital marino
por escalones de agua, por las gradas azules
desciende hasta la arena con pies de luna y lirio.

¡Oh Santa revestida con vellones de oveja!
Les dan una final cura de cielo
a las rocas heridas tus albísimas vendas.

¿De donde tanta nieve caminante,
tantas flores saladas
y despojos de cirios y camisas de ángeles?

¡Oh monja panadera! De cristalinos hornos
fríos de eternidad, sacas infatigable
tus grandes panes blancos y esponjosos.

Despliegas el mantel de un festín de infinito
en donde el horizonte, en su plato de nubes,
sirve el manjar del sueño y del olvido.

También obrera nívea, eres enterradora:
Llevas hasta la arena en paletadas
montones de cadáveres de pálidas gaviotas.

Ruedan sobre la orilla tus vanas esculturas
que pronto se deshacen
en un mármol soluble, én ingrávidas plumas.

Móvil caida nube, al chocar con la tierra
expiras, pero se alza entre las rocas
cual fantasma gaseoso tu presencia.

Arremangado el manto sonante, casta monja
recorres suspirando
tu plantación errante de magnolias.

HERE LIES THE SEAFOAM

The seafoam, sweet nun, in her marine hospital
Descends by staircases of water by blue steps
On feet of moon and lilly to the sand.

Oh Saint, dressed in sheepswool!
Your whitest bandages are a final heavenly cure
For the wounded rocks.

Where does such walking snow come from,
So many salty flowers
And leavings of white candles and shirts of angels?

O, baker nun! From crystaline ovens
Chill with eternity, you take out tirelessly
Your great white spongy loaves.

You unfold the holiday tablecloth of the infinite
On which the horizon, on its plate of clouds,
Serves the refreshments of dream and oblivion.

Likewise, snowy laborer, you are a gravedigger:
You bear to the sand in shovelfuls
Heaps of corpses of pale seagulls.

Your vain sculptures roll over the sand
Soon to melt away
In soluble marble, in weightless feathers.

Mobile, each cloud as it strikes the earth
Expires, but among the rocks there arises
That misty apparition of your presence.

Tucking up your habit, chaste nun,
You sighingly traverse
Your wandering plantation of magnolias.

¿Con material de garzas y medusas
tu flotante y blanquísimo cimiento
va a sostener acaso la ideal arquitectura?

¡Frontera del abismo, guardada por palomas!
Tu ejército nevado avanza hacia la tierra
¡oh monja capitana! en batallas de aurora.

En la arena o las rocas hallas tu fresca tumba;
mas vuelves a nacer a cada instante
y sin pausa atesoras en las conchas tu albura.

De las fieras del mar balsámica saliva
acaricia tus plantas de cristal y de hielo,
¡Santa Espuma difunta en las gradas marinas!

Shaped of herons and medusas
Will your bleached and floating foundation
Perhaps sustain the ideal architecture?

Frontier of the abyss, guarded by doves!
Your snowy army advances toward the land
Oh commanding nun, in battles of sunrise.

In the rocks or the sand you find your cool tomb;
But you are reborn each instant again
And ceaselessly hoard whiteness in the shells.

From the wild beasts of the sea balsamic saliva
Caresses your plants of crystal and ice,
Saint Seafoam, deceased on the steps of the seas!

JUAN SIN CIELO

Juan me llamo, Juan Todos, habitante
de la tierra, más bien su prisionero,
sombra vestida, polvo caminante,
el igual a los otros, Juan Cordero.

Sólo mi mano para cada cosa
— mover la rueda, hallar hondos metales —
mi servidora para asir la rosa
y hacer girar las llaves terrenales.

Mi propiedad labrada en pleno cielo
— un gran lote de nubes era mío —
me pagaba en azul, en paz, en vuelo
y ese cielo en añicos: el rocío.

Mi hacienda era el espacio sin linderos
— oh territorio azul siempre sembrado
de maizales cargados de luceros —
y el rebaño de nubes, mi ganado.

Labradores los pájaros; el día
mi granero de par en par abierto
con mieses y naranjas de alegría.
Maduraba el poniente como un huerto.

Mercaderes de espejos, cazadores
de ángeles llegaron con su espada
y, a cambio de mi hacienda — mar de flores —
me dieron abalorios, humo, nada...

Los verdugos de cisnes, monederos
falsos de las palabras, enlutados,
saquearon mis trojes de luceros,
escombros hoy de luna congelados.

JOHN WITHOUT SKY

John they call me, John Everyman, citizen
Of earth but rather its captive. I go
Dressed in dark garments, trudging in dust,
Similar to all men, I am John Doe.

My hand alone for everything men do —
To move the wheel, to seek out hidden ore —
It is my servant to gather in the rose,
Likewise to turn the key in the world's door.

My land I tilled in the middle of the sky,
Where profits from vast fields of clouds accrue
In blue, in peace and in the flight of birds
And in bright slivers of that sky: the dew.

My hacienda, space without frontiers —
Oh blue expanse, always plowed and seeded
In cornfields, laden with bright stars;
Flocks of clouds were all the herds I needed.

My laborers were the birds and the clear day
Served as my storehouse, always widen open,
Full of harvest grain and oranges of joy
While the west grew ripe as a fruitful garden.

Merchants of mirrors, hunters of angels
Came raging with swords into my lands;
Instead of my acres — a sea of flowers —
They gave glass beads, smoke, nothing-empty hands.

These counterfeiters of words, dressed in black,
These murderers who never spared the swan
Sacked utterly my Troys of brilliant stars
Leaving only frozen debris of the moon.

Perdí mi granja azul, perdí la altura
— reses de nubes, luz recién sembrada —
¡toda una celestial agricultura
en el vacío espacio sepultada!

Del oro del poniente perdí el plano
— Juan es mi nombre, Juan Desposeído —.
En lugar del rocío hallé el gusano
¡un tesoro de siglos he perdido!

Es sólo un peso azul lo que ha quedado
sobre mis hombros, cúpula de hielo...
Soy Juan y nada más, el desolado
herido universal, soy Juan sin Cielo.

I lost my blue granary — cattle of clouds,
Newly sown light — I lost my lofty place,
A whole celestial agriculture ruined,
Buried in the emptiness of space!

I lost the chart, guide to the gold of sunset,
John is my name, John the dispossessed;
Instead of dew I now found only the worm.
I have lost a treasure which centuries amassed.

Only a blue weight is left above me —
Ice cupola on my shoulders — till I die
Plain John forever, the desolate one,
Wounded universally, John without sky.

LA LLAVE DEL FUEGO

¡Tierra equinoccial, patria del colibrí
del árbol de la leche y del árbol del pan!
De nuevo oigo tus grillos y cigarras
moviendo entre las hojas
su herrumbrosa, chirriante maquinaria.
Yo soy el hombre de los papagayos.
Colón me vió en la isla
y me embarcó en su nave de frutas y tesoros
con los pájaros indios para Europa.
Un día, aconsejado por el alba,
desperté las campanas del siglo XIX
y acompañé a Bolívar y sus mendigos héroes
por los países húmedos del eternal verano,
pasé entre la ventisca gris de la cordillera
donde anida el relámpago en su cueva de plata
y más allá hacia el sur,
hacia el círculo máximo del ecuador de fuego
hasta las Capitales de piedras y de nubes
que están cerca del cielo y del rocío.

Yo fundé una república de pájaros
sobre las armaduras de los conquistadores
ya oxidadas de olvido, al pie del bananero.
Sólo resta allí un casco entre la hierba
habitado de insectos como un cráneo vacío
roído eternamente por sus remordimientos.
Me aproximo a las puertas secretas de este mundo
con la llave del fuego
arrancada al volcán solemne como un túmulo.

Te miro, bananero, como a un padre.
Tu alta fábrica verde, alambique del trópico,
tu fresca tubería no descansa
de destilar el tiempo, transmutando

THE KEY OF FIRE

Equinoctial land, fatherland of the hummingbird,
Of the tree of milk, and the breadfruit tree!
Once again I hear your crickets and cicadas
Moving among the leaves
Their rusty, creaking machinery.
I am the man of parrots:
Columbus saw me on the island
And I embarked in his ship of treasure and fruits,
Along with birds of the Indies, for Europe.
One day, counselled by the dawn,
I awoke the bells of the 19th century
And accompanied Bolívar and his beggared heroes
Through the moist countries of eternal summer,
I passed through the grey blizzards of the cordilleras
Where the lighting nestled in its silver cave
And further to the south,
Toward the greatest circle, equator of fire,
To the Capitals of stone and clouds
Situated close to the sky and the dew.

I founded a republic of birds
Upon the armor of the conquistadors
Already rusted with forgetfulness, beneath the banana tree.
All that remained was a helmet in the grass
Inhabited by insects like an empty skull
Eternally gnawed by remorse.
I approached the secret doors of this world
With the key of fire
Snatched from the volcano, solemn as a tomb.

I look on you banana tree as a father.
Your tall green factory, distiler of the tropics,
Your cool pipes never weary
Of distilling time, transmuting

noches en anchas hojas, los días en bananas
o lingotes de sol, dulces cilindros
amasados con flores y con lluvia
en su funda dorada como abeja
o como piel de tigre, olorosa envoltura.

Me sonríe el maíz y habla entre dientes
un lenguaje de agua y de rocío,
el maíz pedagógico que enseña
a contar a los pájaros en su ábaco.
Yo hablo con el maíz y el guacamayo
que conocen la historia del diluvio
cuyo recuerdo nubla la frente de los ríos.
Los ríos adelante corren, siempre adelante
ciñendo, a cada roca, rizada piel de oveja,
hacia los litorales de tortugas,
sin olvidar su origen montañés y celeste
a través del imperio vegetal donde late
la selva con su oscuro corazón de tambor.
¡Oh, mar dulce, Amazonas, y tu fluvial familia!
Disparo mi emplumada flecha o ave mortal
a tu más alta estrella
y busco mi luciente víctima entre tus aguas.

Tierra mía en que habitan razas de la humildad
y el orgullo, del sol y de la luna,
del volcán y del lago, del rayo y los cereales.
En tí existe el recuerdo del fuego elemental
en cada fruto, en cada insecto, en cada pluma,
en el cacto que muestra sus heridas o flores,
en el toro lustroso de candelas y noche,
el mineral insomne bebedor de la luz
y en el caballo rojo que galopa desnudo.
La sequedad arruga los rostros y los muros
y en la extensión de trigo va alumbrando el incendio
su combate de gallos de oro y sangre.

Night into broad leaves, days into bananas,
Or ingots of sun, sweet cylinders
Mouled from flowers and from rain
In their sheaths, gilded like a bee,
Or a tigerskin, perfumed envelopes.

The corn smiles at me and speaks between its teeth
A language of water and dew,
The pedagogical corn which teaches
How to count birds on its abacus.
I speak with the corn and the macaw
Who know the history of the flood,
Whose memory clouds the foreheads of rivers.
The rivers flow onward, always onward,
Girdling each rock, a wrinkled sheepskin,
Toward the shores of turtles,
Never forgetting their mountain and celestial origin
Through all of the vegetable realm where the forest
Beats with its hidden heart of a drum.
Oh sweet sea. Oh Amazon and your flowing family!
I shoot off my plumed arrow or deadly bird
At your highest star
And seek my shining victim among your waters.

My country in which live races full of humility
And pride, and of sun and moon
Of volcano and lake, of thunder and of grain,
In you exists the memory of elemental fire
In each fruit, in each insect, in each feather,
In the cactus which diplays its wounds or flowers,
In the bull, lustrous with candles and night,
In the insomniac mineral, drinker of light
And the red horse galloping naked.
Drought wrinkles faces and walls
And with the expanse of the burning wheatfield illuminates
Its combat of golden cocks and blood.

Yo soy el poseedor de la llave del fuego,
del fuego natural llave pacífica
que abre las invisibles cerraduras del mundo,
la llave del amor y la amapola,
del rubí primordial y la granada,
del cósmico pimiento y de la rosa.
Dulce llave solar que calienta mi mano
extendida a los hombres, sin fronteras:
al de la espada pronta y el guijarro,
al que pesa en balanza la moneda y la flor,
al que tiende un mantel a mi llegada
y al cazador de nubes, maestro de palomas.

Oh, tierra equinoccial de mis antepasados,
cementerio fecundo,
albergue de semillas y cadáveres.
Sobre las momias indias en vasijas de barro
y los conquistadores en sus tumbas de piedra
surcando las edades en su viaje eternal
en compañía sólo de algún insecto músico,
un cielo igual extiende su mirada de olvido.
Zarpa un nuevo Colón entre las nubes
mientras estalla, breve fuego mudo,
la pólvora celeste del lucero
y los inquietos gritos de los pájaros.
son oscuras preguntas al ocaso.

I am the possessor of the key of fire,
Of natural peaceful fire,
Which opens the invisible locks of the world,
The key of love and of the poppy
Of the primordial ruby and the pomegranate
Of the cosmic red pepper and the rose.
Sweet solar key which warms my hand
Extended to all men beyond frontiers:
To the man of the quick sword and the pebble,
He who weighs money and flower in the scales,
He who spreads a tablecloth for my arrival
And to the hunter of clouds, master of doves.

Oh equinoctial land of my forebears,
Fecund cemetery,
Lodging of seed and corpses.
Over the Indian mummies and vessels of clay
And the conquistadors in their stone tombs,
Furrowing the ages in their eternal journey
Accompanied only with some musical insect,
An impartial sky extends its forgetful stare.
A new Columbus sets sails among the clouds,
While the briel mute fire
The celestial gunpowder of the morning star explodes
And the inquiet cries of the birds
Are obscure questions asked of the sunset.

FAMILIA DE NOCHE
1952-1953

FAMILIA DE LA NOCHE

I

Si entro por esta puerta veré un rostro
ya desaparecido, en un clima de pájaros.
Avanzará a mi encuentro
hablándome con sílabas de niebla,
en un país de tierra transparente
donde medita sin moverse el tiempo
y ocupan su lugar los seres y las cosas
en un orden eterno.

Si contemplo este árbol, desde el fondo
de los años saldrá una voz dormida,
voz de ataúd y oruga
explicando los días
que a su tronco y sus hojas hincharon de crepúsculos
ya maduros de hormigas en la tumba
donde la Dueña de las Golondrinas
oye la eterna música.

¿Es con tu voz nutrida de luceros,
gallo, astrólogo ardiente,
que entreabres la cancela de la infancia?
¿O acaso es tu sonámbula herradura,
caballo anacoreta del establo,
que repasa en el sueño los caminos
y anuncia con sus golpes en la sombra
la cita puntual del alba y del rocío?

Estación del maíz salvado de las aguas:
La mazorca, Moisés vegetal en el río
iba a lavar su estirpe fundadora de pueblos
y maduraba su oro protegido por lanzas.
Parecían los asnos
volver de Tierra Santa,

FAMILY OF NIGHT

I

If I go through this door I shall see a face,
Which has already disappeared, in a climate of birds.
It will come to meet me
Speaking to me in syllabes of mist.
In a country of transparent earth
Where time meditates motionless
And things and beings take their places
In an eternal order.

If I contemplate this tree, from the depth
Of the years a sleepy voice will rise up
A caterpillar and coffin voice
Explaining the days
Which swell its leaves and trunk with twilights,
Already ripe with ants in the tomb
Where the Mistress of Swallows
Listens to eternal music.

Is it with your voice nourished with morning stars,
Cock, ardent astrologer,
That you have opened the screendoor of childhood?
Or perhaps it is your somnabulent horseshoes,
Hermit horse in the stable,
Revisiting roads in dreams
With your blows in the darkness announcing
The punctual appointments of dawn and dew?

Season of corn saved from the waters:
The ear of corn, a vegetable Moses went to wash
Its lineage, the founder of peoples,
And to ripen its gold protected by lances.
Donkeys appeared
To return to the Holy Land,

asns uniformados de silencio
y de polvo, vendiendo mansedumbre en canastas.

Grecia, en el palomar daba lecciones
de alada ciencia. Formas inventaban,
celeste geometría,
las palomas alumnas de la luz.
Egipto andaba en los escarabajos
y en los perros perdidos que convoca la noche
a su asamblea de almas y de piedras.
Yo, primer hombre, erraba entre las flores.

En esa noche de oro
que en pleno día teje la palmera
me impedían dormir, Heráclito, tus pasos
que sin fin recomienzan.
Las ruinas aprendían de memoria
la odisea cruel de los insectos,
y los cuervos venidos de las rocas
me traían el pan del evangelio.

Un dios lacustre andaba entre los juncos
soñando eternidades
y atesorando cielos bajo el agua.
La soledad azul contaba pájaros.
Dándome la distancia en un mugido
el toro me llamaba de la orilla.
Sus pisadas dejaban en la tierra
en cuencos de agua idénticos, muertas mitologías.

En su herrería aérea las campanas
martillaban espadas rotas de la Edad Media.
Las nubes extendían nuevos mapas
de tierras descubiertas.
Y a mediodía, en su prisión de oro,
el monarca de plumas

Donkeys, uniformed in silence
And dust, selling humility in baskets.

In the dovecote Greece gave lessons
In winged science. Doves,
Alumnae of light, invented shapes
Celestial geometry.
Egypt appeared in the scarabs
And lost dogs which gathered at night
In their assembly of souls and stones.

I, the first man, wandered among the flowers.
In this golden night
What in daylight weaves the palmtree
Kept me from sleeping, Heraclitus your steps
Endlessly beginning again.
Ruins have learned from memory
The cruel odessey of insects,
And the crows coming from the rocks
Brought me evangelical bread.

A lacustrine god walked among the reeds
Dreaming eternities
And hoarding skies beneath the water.
Blue solitude counted birds.
Measuring distance for me by his bellow
The bull called to me from the shore.
His hoofprints left behind in the earth
In identical pools of water, mythological deaths.

In their airy ironwork the bells
Hammered broken swords of the Middle Ages.
The clouds extended new maps
Of discovered lands.
And at midday in his golden prison
The monarch of feathers

le pedía a la muerte que leyera
el nombre de ese Dios escrito sobre la uña.

Colón y Magallanes vivían en una isla
al fondo de la huerta
y todos los salvajes del crepúsculo
sus plumajes quemaban en la celeste hoguera.
¿Qué queda de los fúlgidos arneses
y los nobles caballos de los conquistadores?
¡Sólo lluvia en los huesos carcomidos
y un relincho de historia a medianoche!

En el cielo fluía el Amazonas
con ribereñas selvas de horizonte.
Orellana zarpaba cada día
en su viaje de espumas y tambores
y la última flecha de la luz
hería mi ojo atento,
fray Gaspar de las nubes, cronista del ocaso
en esa expedición fluvial del sueño.

Por el cerro salía en procesión la lluvia
en sus andas de plata.
El agua universal pasaba la frontera
y el sol aparecía prisionero entre lanzas.
Mas, el sordo verano por sorpresa
ocupaba el país a oro y fuego
y asolaban poblados y caminos
Generales de polvo con sus tropas de viento.

II

Tu geografía, infancia, es la meseta
de los Andes, entera en mi ventana
y ese río que va de fruta en roca
midiendo a cada cosa la cintura

Begged that death would read
The name of that God written on his nail.

Columbus and Magellan lived on an island
At the back of the garden
And all the savages of twilight
Burned their feather dresses in the celestial bonfire.
What is left of gleaming harnesses
And the noble steeds of the conquistadors?
Only rain upon wormeaten bones
And a neighing out of history at midnight!

The Amazon flowed through the sky
With wooded shores of horizon.
Orellana set sail every day
On his voyage of foam and drums
And the last arrow of light
Wounded my staring eye,
Friar Gaspar of the clouds, cronicler of sunset
On that river expedition of dream.

From the peaks rain came in a procession
Carried on its silver litters.
Universel water passed beyond the frontier
And the sun seemed imprisoned by lances.
But deaf summer in surprise attack
Occupied the country with gold and fire
While villages and roadways were laid waste
By generals of dust with their troops of wind.

II

Your geography, childhood, is the plateau
Of the Andes, which reports through my window
And that river which goes from fruit and rock
Measuring the girth of everything

y hablando en un lenguaje de guijarros
que repiten las hojas de los árboles.
En los montes despierta el fuego planetario
y el dios del rayo come los cereales.

¡Alero del que parten tantas alas!
¡Albarda del tejado con su celeste carga!
El campo se escondía en los armarios
y en todos los espejos se miraba.
Yo recibía al visitante de oro
que entraba, matinal por la ventana
y se iba, oscurecido, pintándote de ausencia
¡alero al que regresan tantas alas!

En esa puerta, madre, tu estatura
medías, hombro a hombro, con la tarde
y tus manos enviaban golondrinas
a tus hijos ausentes
preguntando noticias a las nubes,
oyendo las pisadas del ocaso
y haciendo enmudecer con tus suspiros
los gritos agoreros de los pájaros.

¡Madre de la alegría de la tierra,
nodriza de palomas,
inventora del sueño que consuela!
Madrugadores días, aves, cosas
su desnudez vestían de inocencia
y en tus ojos primero amanecían
antes de concurrir a saludarnos
con su aire soleado de familia.

Imitaban las plantas y los pájaros
tus humildes afanes. Y la caña de azúcar
nutría su raíz más secreta en tu sien,
manantial primigenio de dulzura.
A un gesto de tus manos milagrosas

And speaking in the language of pebbles
Which repeat the leaves of the trees.
Planetary fire awakens in the mountains
And the god of lightning eats the grain.

Eaves from which so many wings departed!
Halbard of tile with its airy cargo!
The country hid itself in the wardrobes
And all the mirrors looked at each other.
I received the golden visitor
Entering each morning through the window
And leaving, shadowed, painting you with absence,
Eaves to which so many wings returned!

In that doorway, mother, your figure
Measured twilight, shoulder to shoulder,
And your hands sent out swallows
To your absent sons
Asking news of the clouds,
Listening to the steps of sunset
And silencing with your sighs
The prophetic cries of the birds.

Mother of the earth's joy,
Wetnurse to doves,
Inventor of consoling sleep!
Dawn-rising days, birds, things,
Their nakedness dressed in innocence
And in your eyes, they first appeared
Before they met to greet us
With their sunburnt family look.

Plants and birds imitated
Your humble solicitude. And the sugarcane
Nourished its most secret root in your breast,
Primal shower of sweetness.
A gesture of your miraculous hands

el dios de la alacena te entregaba sus dones.
Madre de las manzanas
y del pan, Madre augusta de las trojes.

¡Devuélveme el mensaje de los tordos!
No puedo vivir más sin el topacio
del día ecuatorial.
¡Dáme la flor que gira desde el alba al ocaso,
yacente Dueña de las Golondrinas!
¿Dónde está la corona de abundancia
que lucían los campos? Ya sólo oro
difunto en hojarasca pisoteada.

III

Aquí desciendes, padre, cada tarde
del caballo luciente como el agua
con espuma de marcha y de fatiga.
Nos traes la ciudad bien ordenada
en números y rostros: el mejor de los cuentos.
Tu frente resplandece como el oro,
patriarca, hombre de ley, de cuyas manos
nacen las cosas en su sitio propio.

Cada hortaliza o árbol,
cada teja o ventana, te deben su existencia.
Levantaste tu casa en el desierto,
correr hiciste el agua, ordenaste la huerta,
padre del palomar y de la cuadra,
del pozo doctoral y del umbroso patio.
En tu mesa florida de familia
reía tu maíz solar de magistrado.

Mas, la muerte, de pronto
entró en el patio espantando las palomas
con su caballo gris y su manto de polvo.

The god of the cupboard bestowed its gifts upon you.
Mother of apples
And of bread, august Mother of granaries.

Restore the message of the thrushes to me.
I can no longer live without the topaz
Of the ecuatorial day.
Give me the flower that turns from dawn to sunset,
Reclining Mistress of Swallows!
Where is the crown of abundance
That shone in the fields? Now there's only
Dead gold in the trodden dead leaves.

III

Here you dismount every day, father,
From the horse that shines like water
From the froth of weariness and travel.
You bring us the orderly city
Of faces and numbers: the best stories.
Your forehead gleaming like gold,
Patriarch, man of law, from whose hand
Things are born their proper place.

Each vegetable or tree
Every tile or window owes its existence to you.
You raised your house in the desert,
You made water flow, you set out the garden
Father of the dovecote and the stable
Of the learned well and the shady patio.
On your flowering family table
In you, a sunny lawgiver, the maize laughed.

But death, suddenly
Entered the patio frightening the doves
With its grey horse and mantle of dust.

Azucenas y sábanas, entre luces atónitas,
de nieve funeral
el dormitorio helaron de la casa.
Y un rostro se imprimió para siempre en la noche
como una hermosa máscara.

Es el pozo, privado de sus astros
noche en profundidad, cielo vacío,
y el palomar y huerta ya arrasados
se llaman noche, olvido.
Bolsa de aire no más, noche con plumas
es el muerto pichón. Se llama noche
el paisaje abolido. Sólo orugas habitan
la noche de ese rostro yacente entre las flores.

Honeysuckle and bedsheets, among astonished lights,
In the bedroom of the house
Congealed with snowy funeral.
And a face was imprinted on the night forever
Like a beautiful mask.

The pool deprived of its stars is
Profound night, empty sky,
And the dovecote and the orchard now razed
Are called night, oblivion.
The dead pigeon is
Nothing but a bag of air.
A feathered night. The erased landscape
Is called night. Only caterpillars live in
The night of this face stretched out among the flowers.

DICTADO POR EL AGUA

I

Aire de soledad, dios transparente
que en secreto edificas tu morada
¿en pilares de vidrio de qué flores?
¿sobre la galería iluminada
de qué río, qué fuente?
Tu santuario es la gruta de colores.
Lengua de resplandores
hablas, dios escondido,
al ojo y al oído.
Sólo en la planta, el agua, el polvo asomas
con tu vestido de alas de palomas
despertando el frescor y el movimiento.
En tu caballo azul van los aromas,
Soledad convertida en elemento.

II

Fortuna de cristal, cielo en monedas,
agua, con tu memoria de la altura,
por los bosques y prados
viajas con tus alforjas de frescura
que guardan por igual las arboledas
y las hierbas, las nubes y ganados.
Con tus pasos mojados
y tu piel de inocencia
señalas tu presencia
hecha toda de lágrimas iguales,
agua de soledades celestiales.
Tus peces son tus ángeles menores
que custodian tesoros eternales
en tus frías bodegas interiores.

DICTATED BY THE WATER

I

Air, transparent and lonely god,
You, who build your dwelling in secret,
In pillars of glass of what flowers.
Above the illuminated gallery
Of what river, what spring?
Your sanctuary is formed in a grotto of color.
You speak a language of splendors,
God, hidden
From sight and hearing.
Only from the plant, the water, the dust
Do you peep out in your dress of doves' wings
Awaking coolness and movement.
Perfumes ride on your blue horse,
Solitude converted into an element.

II

Crystal fortune, sky of coins,
Water, with your memory of height,
Through woods and fields you travel
With your saddlebags of coolness
Protecting impartially groves
And grass, clouds and cattle.
With your moist steps
And your innocent skin
You manifest your presence
Formed wholly of similar tears,
Water of celestial solitudes.
Your fish are your minor angels
Who guard eternal treasures
In your cold interior storerooms.

III

Doncel de soledad, oh lirio armado
por azules espadas defendido,
gran señor con tu vara de fragancia,
a los cuentos del aire das oído.
A tu fiesta de nieve convidado
el insecto aturdido de distancia
licor de cielo escancia,
maestro de embriagueces
solitarias a veces.
Mayúscula inicial de la blancura:
De retazos de nube y agua pura
está urdido tu cándido atavío
donde esplenden, nacidos de la altura
huevecillos celestes del rocío.

IV

Sueñas, magnolia casta, en ser paloma
o nubecilla enana, suspendida
sobre las hojas, luna fragmentada.
Solitaria inocencia recogida
en un nimbo de aroma.
Santa de la blancura inmaculada.
Soledad congelada
hasta ser alabastro
tumba, lámpara o astro,
Tu oronda frente que la luz ampara
es del candor del mundo la alquitara
donde esencia secreta extrae el cielo.
En nido de hojas que el verdor prepara,
esperas resignada el don del vuelo.

III

Young page of solitude, oh, armed lilly,
Defended by blue swords,
Great lord with your staff of fragrance,
You give utterance to the tales of the air.
Invited to your snowy fiesta,
The insect, giddy with distance,
Serves liquor of sky,
Master of drunkenness
Sometimes solitary.
Capital letter, initial of whiteness:
Your shining raiment is contrived
Of strips of cloud and pure water
Where, born of height, tiny celestial
Eggs of dew shimmer.

IV

You dream, chaste magnolia, of being dove
Or dwarf cloud, suspended
Over the leaves, a shattered moon.
Solitary innocence, gathered
In a nimbus of perfume.
Saint of immaculate whiteness.
Solitude frozen
Until it is alabaster
Tombstone, lamp or star.
Your rounded forehead protected by light
Is the whiteness of the world, the alembic
Where the sky extracts a secret essence.
In a nest of leaves prepared by verdure,
You patiently await the gift of flight.

V

Flor de amor, flor de ángel, flor de abeja,
cuerpecillos medrosos, virginales
con pies de sombra, amortajados vivos,
ángeles en pañales.
El rostro de la dalia tras su reja,
los nardos que arden en su albura, altivos,
los jacintos cautivos
en su torre delgada
de aromas fabricada,
girasoles, del oro buscadores:
lenguas de soledad, todas las flores
niegan o asienten según habla el viento
y en la alquimia fugaz de los olores
preparan su fragante acabamiento.

VI

¡De murallas que viste el agua pura
y de cúpula de aves coronado
mundo de alas, prisión de transparencia
donde vivo encerrado!
Quiere entrar la verdura
por la ventana a pasos de paciencia,
y anuncias tu presencia
con tu cesta de frutas, lejanía.
Mas, cumplo cada día,
Capitán del color, antiguo amigo
de la tierra mi límpido castigo.
Soy a la vez cautivo y carcelero
de esta celda de cal que anda conmigo,
de la que, oh muerte, guardas el llavero

V

Flower of love, angelflower, beeflower,
Tiny timorous virginal bodies
With feet of shadow, enshrouded alive,
Angels in swaddling clothes.
The face of the dahlia through its grating,
The tuberoses that burn in their proud whiteness,
The captive hyacinths
In their slender tower
Manufactured of perfume,
Sunflowers, gold prospectors:
Tongues of solitude, all the flowers
Disagree or agree, as the wind speaks
And in the fleeting alchemy of perfumes
Prepare their own fragrant extinction.

VI

I live enclosed
By walls formed of pure water
By a cupola crowned by birds,
A world of wings, a prison of transparency.
The green foliage wishes to enter
By the window, on steps of patience,
And you announce your presence
With your tray of fruit, distance.
But I complete each day,
As Captain of color, old friend.
Of the earth, my limpid punishment;
I am at the same time captive and jailer
Of this celle of lime which travels with me,
And of which, oh death, you keep the key.

LAS ARMAS DE LA LUZ

I

El día, alzado en armas,
gira a mi alrededor ¡oh cerco de oro
seguido por la azul caballería
del horízonte en trance de palabra
o de vocal redonda eternamente!
¡Del paladar de nubes, oh bostezo,
oh suspiro entre rocas amarillas
y emboscados ejércitos solares!
Me entrego al sitiador esplendoroso,
prisionero de sombra sin combate,
rendido a la evidencia meridiana,
omnipresente en árbol, roca, insecto,
paraíso terrestre renovado
cada día del mundo, sin la fábula,
en las cosas dispersas libremente,
cuya sola presencia es un mensaje
en idioma de luz que me penetra.
La luz hace nacer todas las formas,
extranjera venida de la altura
palabra de lo eterno repetida,
hasta el fin de los siglos siempre virgen,
más vieja, sin embargo, que las piedras
o que los animales o las plantas,
madre del universo pasajera
de planeta en planeta, que por turno
se animan al amor de su mirada.

II

La luz me mira: existo. La luz mira
en torno mío todo, hasta el guijarro,

WEAPONS OF LIGHT

I

The day risen in arms,
Spins about me, oh ring of gold
Followed by the blue cavalry
Of the horizon that seems about to speak
Or pronounce the eternally rounded vowel!
Oh yawn from the throat of the clouds,
Oh sigh among yellow rocks
And ambuscaded armies of sun!
I surrender to the splendid besieger.
Without hostilities, prisoner of shadow,
Giving myself up on the midday evidence
Omnipresent in the tree, the rock, the insect,
Each day a terrestrial paradise renewed
In this world, without fable,
In the things freely spread about
Whose presence alone is a message
Penetrating me with an idiom of light.
The light gives birth to all shapes,
A stranger come from above,
Repetition of the eternal word
Always virgin until the end of the centuries,
Yet older than the stones
Or the animals or the plants.
Mother of the universe, traveller
From planet to planet, each in turn
Animated by the love in your glance.

II

The light looks at me: I exist. The light
Looks at everything round me even to the pebble.

y cada árbol afirma su existencia
por sus hojas sumisas, que se bañan
en la total mirada de la altura.
Un río lleva en su alma esa mirada
que borrar con azul en vano intentan
piedrecillas o ramas que se hunden
y hacen sólo surgir entre las aguas
la forma del gran ojo que se abre
al turbar la dormida transparencia.
Horizonte de rocas o molares
de Dios, en donde habita la palabra
profunda: más allá. ¡Vocablo de oro
en la hueca garganta de distancia!
Ya comprendo la lengua de lo eterno,
como de lo lejano y lo escondido;
porque la luz ha entrado meridiana
en mi cuerpo de sombra hasta los huesos,
tubería de cal por donde sopla
la música del mundo, el tierno cántico
de la familia universal de seres
en la unidad terrena, planetaria
de su común origen: la luz madre.

III

Translúcida la avispa, prisionera
de su ámbito floral, comprueba al vuelo
su libertad medida, su dominio
cercado por las huestes vegetales
y en su mundo de sol gira gozosa,
angélica en su cielo de hojas y aire,
y fabrica dulzura sin descanso
con materia de luz su oro gustoso,
guardiana de su mágica alquitara
con su lanza de fuego va volando,

And each tree affirms its existence
By its submissive leaves, bathing
In the all-embracing glance from above.
A river carries this glance in its soul
Which little stones or branches try
Vainly to blot out with blue, and they sink
And simply force up through the waters
The shape of the great eye which opens
As the sleeping transparency is disturbed.
Horizon of rocks or God's molars in which
The profound word lives: far beyond. Golden vocable
In the hollow throat of distance!
Now I understand the eternal language
Like that of the far distant and the hidden
Because the light at midday had entered
My body of shadow even to the bones.
Limy pipes through which blows
The music of the world, a gentle canticle
Of the universal family of beings
In the unity of the earth, planetary
In its common origin: the maternal light.

III

The translucent wasp, prisoner
In its floral neighbor hood, confirms
Its limited freedom in flight, its kingdom
Fenced in by vegetable hosts
And in its world of sun circles joyfully,
Angelically, in its sky full of leaves and air,
And fabricates sweetness, tirelessly
Its delicious gold made from light,
Guardian of its magic alembic
With a lance of fire, it goes flying,
A minute amazon, armed with honey.

minúscula amazona, miel armada.
Avispa cazadora y mensajera,
cínifes transparentes como el aire,
insectos de la luz, familia diáfana
o signos de una efímera escritura
en texto natural para los pájaros
que leen entre silbos, tragan letras
caídas en la hierba o seres vivos,
jinetes desmontados en la guerra
de siglos que comienza cada día,
guerra civil terrestre de gusanos
que devora el Gran Mirlo de la sombra.

IV

Sólo es luz emplumada el colibrí,
luz con alas o mínima saeta
que las flores se lanzan una a otra
al corazón de aroma y de rocío.
Le ve pasar el aire en un relámpago
de pedrería cálida, volante
astilla de vitral, reflejo de agua,
fugas en el espejo del espacio
que le mira incansable pasajero
ir y venir, imagen de la prisa
entre la lentitud grave del mundo
en la solar batalla meridiana
y buscar vanamente la flor Única
en su breve estación sobre la tierra
hasta que el pico encuentra en la corola
el azúcar secreto de la muerte.
Mas, la herencia del pájaro difunto
se reparten insectos y raíces
y el color de las alas va a los frutos,
miniaturas del sol, planetas dulces,

Wasp, huntress and messenger,
Mosquitos transparent as the air,
Insects of light, diaphanous family,
Or signs of an ephemeral writing
In a text familiar to the birds
who read between syllables, swallow letters
Fallen to the grass or living beings,
Dismounted horsemen in the war
Of centuries which begin each day,
Earthly civil war of the worms
Which the Great Blackbird of shadow devours.

IV

The hummingbird is nothing but plumed light.
Light with wings or at least a dart
Which the flowers throw at each other
At the heart of perfume and of dew.
I see it pass through the air, a streak of lightning.
Of red hot jewels, a flying
Spark of glass, a reflection of water
Fleeting in the mirror of space
Which stares at it, tireless traveller
Coming and going, image of speed.
Amidst the grave sluggishness of the world
Engaged in the midday battle of sun,
Seeking vainly the Unique flower
During its brief season on earth
Until its beak encounters in the corolla
The secret sugar of death.
But the heritage of the departed bird
Is divided by insects and roots
And the color of the wings goes to the fruit,
Miniature suns, sweet planets,
And from thence returns once more in golden pulp.

y de allí nuevamente en pulpa de oro
o en sangre vegetal, licor nutricio,
a la tribu del aire y de la pluma
en un ciclo infinito de animales
y semillas, de insectos y de plantas
que gobierna la luz, la luz suprema.

V

Amistad de las cosas y los seres
en apariencia solos y distintos
pero en su vida cósmica enlazados
en oscura, esencial correspondencia
más allá de sus muertes, a otras formas
del existir terrestre a grandes pasos
hacia el gris mineral inexorable.
Su alimento de luz para ese tránsito
cada día del mundo lo recogen
— desde el pez que lo cambia en plata pura
hasta la golondrina que lo esconde
bajo el tejado, paja a paja de oro,
o el peral en sus pálidas redomas —
todos los seres de agua, tierra y aire,
especies interinas, vestiduras
mortales, sucesivas, de lo eterno.
En la escala que sube del guijarro
a la escama, a la hoja y a la pluma
una armonía pávida interroga,
dividida en millares de preguntas
que repiten los ecos papagayos.

VI

¡Cielo entre cuatro rocas solas: háblame!
Tu boca desdentada ya modula

In blood of plants, nourishing liquor,
To the tribes of the air and of feathers
In an infinite cycle of animals
And seeds, of insects and plants
Governed by light, the supreme light.

V

Friendship of things and beings
In appearance separate and distinct,
But interwoven in their cosmic existence
In dark essential correspondence
Beyond their deaths, with other forms
Of earthly life, in great steps
Toward the grey, inexorable mineral.
Each day on earth they gather
Their food of light for this passage —
From the fish which changes it to pure silver
To the swallow which hides it
Beneath the tiles, straw by golden straw,
Or the pear in its pale vial —
All beings of water, earth and air,
Temporary species, mortal vestments,
And successive, of the eternal.
In the series which rises from the pebble
To the scale, the leaf and the feather
A timid harmony puts its queries,
Divided into millions of questions
Repeated by echos like parrots.

VI

Sky between four lonely rocks, speak to me!
Your toothless mouth already modifies

el tremendo secreto meridiano.
Mente sin nubes, diáfana conciencia
transmíteme la idea en llama pura.
Tu elocuencia de miel solar me envuelve
y nace en mí la fúlgida evidencia.
¿Quién soy? ¿En dónde estoy? El mediodía
me circunda con su oro, mina inmensa.
Soy soldado del lirio y de la avispa
y servidor simétrico del mundo;
tengo un ojo de sol y otro de sombra,
un punto cardinal en cada mano
y ando, miro y trabajo doblemente
mientras dos veces peso en la balanza
cerebral en secreto
el vinagre y la miel de cada cosa.
Mido el tiempo, el color, mi metro aplico
a lo que me rodea, mas no veo
más allá de las nubes, se me escapan
la música y la luz entre los dedos.

VII

Obeso mediodía, de topacios
nutrido, siempre ardiente de sed alta,
soberano absoluto de un imperio
de doradas arenas infinitas:
Tu batalla ganada la contempla
la azul caballería
del horizonte, pronta a entrar en fuego.
¡Oh frescas emboscadas de la sombra
para apresar las huestes meridianas
en sus trampas de vidrios y de insectos!
Allí donde hay un árbol o una fuente
pende o flota una víctima radiosa.
Mas el oro del cielo,

The tremendous midday secret.
Mins without clouds, diaphanous conscience,
Impart the idea to me in pure flame.
Your eloquence of sunlit honey surrounds me
And the glowing evidence is born in me.
Who am I? Where am I? The midday
Encircles me with its gold, an immense mine.
I am soldier of the lilly and the wasp
And symmetrical servitor of the world;
I have an eye of sun and another of shade,
A point of the compass in each hand
And I walk, I look and work twofold
While I twice weigh on the cerebral
And secret scale
The vinegar and honey of everything.
I measure time, color, I apply my unit
To what surrounds me, but I see
No further than the clouds; music and light
Both escape from between my fingers.

VII

Obese midday, nourished
On topazes, always burning with a lofty thirst,
Absolute sovereign of an empire
Of infinite gilded sands:
Your battle won, the blue cavalry
Of the horizon contemplates it
Soon to burst into flame.
Oh cool ambushes of shade
Ready to imprison the midday hosts
In your pitfalls of insects and glass!
Yonder wherever there is a tree or spring
A radiant victim hangs or floats.
But the gold of the sky

en ofensiva unánime
de cornetas solares y de viento,
ocupa el territorio. Libres andan
en el gran campamento de la luz
los hombres en recreo de cautivos
entre los que ando solo, con mi avispa,
mis dos sombras — la grande y la del suelo —
mi costumbre de hablar a cada cosa
y beber sorbo a sorbo el tiempo inmenso
hasta que el día entero se consume
y veo amontonarse en el ocaso
las armas de la luz ensangrentadas.
En mi morada oscura
vuelvo a escuchar al hombre del espejo
que habla conmigo a solas,
me mira e interroga frente a frente
en eco me responde en mi lenguaje
y se asemeja a mí más que yo mismo.

In an all-out offensive
Of troups of sun and of wind
Occupies the territory. In the great
Encampment of light
Men walk free, exercising like prisoners
Among whom I walk alone, with my wasp,
My two shadows — the tall one and the one on the ground —
And my habit of talking to everything
And drinking, sip by sip, the immensity of time
Until the whole day is consumed
And I see heaped up in the west
The bloody weapons of the light.
In my dark dwelling
I once more listen to the man in the mirror
Who talks to me alone.
Looks at me and questions me, face to face,
Who answers me with an echo in my own language
And resembles me more than I do myself.

HOMBRE PLANETARIO
1957-1963

INVECTIVA CONTRA LA LUNA

Yo podría decir: Luna, fruto de hielo
en las ramas azules de la noche.
Pero tantos sollozos se esconden en las piedras,
tantos combates mudos se libran en la sombra,
que yo digo: la luna es sólo un pozo
de llanto de los hombres.

Tantas lágrimas ruedan por las tumbas,
tantas lágrimas corren por el hambre
de ojos ya sin edad, desde hace siglos,
que la lluvia no cesa sobre el mundo,
y yo veo tan sólo la harina de la luna
y su plato vacio y su mortaja.

Yo podría decir: La luna es una mina
de plata fabulosa,
la luna de paseo va con sus guantes blancos
a coger margaritas. Pero hay tantos difuntos
sin flores, tantos niños con las manos heladas,
que yo digo: La luna es el Polo del cielo.

Bruja azul, encantaba el sueño de los hombres,
inventaba el primer amor de las doncellas,
andaba por los bosques con chinelas de vidrio
en los tiempos felices. La luna era una almohada
de plumas arrancadas a los ángeles
para dormir la eternidad celeste.

Luna: arroja tu máscara en el agua,
reparte tus harinas, tus sábanas, tus panes
entre todos los hombres.
No seas sólo un pozo de lágrimas, un témpano
o un islote de sal, sino un granero
para el hambre infinita de la tierra.

INVECTIVE AGAINST THE MOON

I could say: moon, icy fruit
On the blue branches of the night.
But so many sobs are hidden in the stones,
So many mute conflicts are loosed in the shadows
That I say: the moon is only a pool
For human tears.

So many tears around graveyards,
So many tears flow from hunger,
From ageless eyes, for centuries,
The rain that never ceases on this earth.
And all I see is the moon's white flour,
Its empty plate and its winding sheet.

I could say: the moon is a mine
Of fabulous silver,
The moon promenades in its white gloves
On its way to pick daisies. But so many dead
Lack flowers; so many children have icy hands
That I say: the moon is the North Pole of the sky.

Blue sorceress, she enchanted the sleep of men,
She invented the young girl's first love
And strayed through the forest in glass slippers
In times of joy. The moon was a cushion
Stuffed with fathers snatched from angels
To put celestial eternity to sleep.

Moon, take off your mask in the water,
Distribute your white flour, your blankets, your bread
Among all mankind.
Be no longer a pool of tears, an iceberg,
An island of salt, but a granary
For the infinite hunger of the earth.

AUROSIA

Todo es oro en Aurosia, el remoto planeta
donde las noches áureas son más claras que el día.
Los seres que lo habitan, más humanos que el hombre,
viven en paz cavando sus auríferas minas.

Planeta venturoso, Nuevo Mundo sin fieras
ni miedo, sin vejez ni angustia de la mente.
Jóvenes de cien años, vigorosos y lúcidos,
en los jardines de oro van a esperar la muerte.

Todo es libre en Aurosia: el agua, el aire, el suelo.
Hasta el trigo es silvestre y el pan es para todos.
Máquinas silenciosas andan, cavan, construyen,
producen luz, transforman en mil cosas el oro.

Aurosia es un planeta de gigantes magnánimos
siempre risueños; forman una sola familia,
una sola nación sin inventos de muerte,
y es de color de sol su bandera pacífica.

Nautas de los espacios, visitan otros mundos
y el mapa de los cielos conocen de memoria.
Amigos de las aves y los ínfimos seres,
cultivan flores de oro con manos amorosas.

Adanes del azul, más perfectos que el hombre,
dueños de un paraíso planetario
donde las madres siempre son jóvenes y vírgenes
en su reino de fuentes, de manzanas y pájaros.

Las mujeres de Aurosia tienen un cuerpo de oro.
Son cántaros de miel con gargantas de música.
En sus hombros de luz y en sus senos de ídolos
hay flores en balanzas, hay metales y plumas.

AUROSIA

All is golden in Aurosia, that distant planet
Where golden nights are clearer than the day.
The beings who live there, more human than men,
Live in peace, digging in their goldmines.

Fortunate planet, New World without carnivores,
Nor fear, nor old age nor minds full of anxiety,
Youths of a hundred years, clear-headed and vigorous,
In golden gardens go to wait for death.

All is free in Aurosia, the soil, the air, the water,
Even wheat grows wild and there's bread for everyone.
Silent machines move, mine and fabricate
Produce light, transform the gold into a thousand things.

Aurosia is a planet of magnanimous giants,
Always smiling, they belong to a single family,
A single nation without death dealing weapons
And their peaceful flag is the color of sunlight.

Sailors of space, they go visiting other worlds
And they know the map of the heavens by heart.
Friends of the birds and of the most infinitesimal beings,
With hands of love they cultivate golden flowers.

Adams from the sky, more perfect than mankind,
They are masters of a planetary paradise
Where mothers remain forever virgin and youthful
In their domain of foutains, apples and songbirds.

The bodies of the women of Aurosia are golden.
They are jars of honey, with throats full of music,
Shoulders of lights, in their breasts like idols
There are scales laden with flowers, metals and feathers.

131

Desde Aurosia, les niños pueden mirar la Tierra
y saben nuestra historia increíble: las razas
que se odian, la sed del oro, la conquista
y exterminio de pueblos al filo de la espada.

¡Tierra: planeta viejo, atrasado en el cosmos
con millones de años, refugio de los seres
más primarios y mínimos del universo, hormigas
del azul, debatiéndose bajo el pie de la muerte!

La distancia entre Aurosia y la Tierra se mide
no sólo en años-luz a través de la nada,
sino en años-amor, en siglos de ternura.
No es capaz el terrícola de salvar la distancia.

Aurosia, Nuevo Mundo sin ofidios ni flechas:
el gozo de vivir corre en tus manantiales.
Nadie ha visto una lágrima en la historia de Aurosia.
(Hay una en el museo, convertida en diamante.)

Los árboles de Aurosia dan más frutos que hojas
cuatro veces al año. Hay cuatro lunas llenas
en el cielo sin nubes,
y se ven cuatro veces más astros que en la Tierra.

From Aurosia children can look earthward
And learn our incredible history, of various races
Hating each other, thirst for gold, our conquests
And extermination of peoples with the edge of the sword.

Earth, aged planet, cosmically backward
With your millions of years, refuge of beings
most primitive, most minimal in the universe, ants
Of the firmament, debating on the brink of death!

The distance between Aurosia and the earth is measured
Not only in light-years across nothingness
But in love-years, in centuries of tenderness,
A terrestrial can not conceive this distance.

Aurosia, New World without poison — snakes or arrows.
An appetite for living flows in your spring torrents.
In all Aurosia's history no one has seen a tear;
(There is one in the museum preserved as a diamond.)

The trees of Aurosia bear more fruit than leaves
Four times a year, there are four full moons
In a cloudless sky, and there can be seen
Four times as many stars as we see from earth.

TALLER DEL TIEMPO

Herrero del otoño: forja mi corazón,
da forma a su racimo en tu yunque de oro.
A cada golpe gime el metal del olvido.
Al soplo de la fragua arden hasta las nubes.

Soy un hombre vestido de hojas secas.
Mi pecho abriga líquenes de fuentes extinguidas.
El pájaro hablador de otro tiempo cantaba:
"El mundo es tuyo. Tómalo. La luz marca tu frente."

Yo te grité mi amor, Naturaleza impávida,
ciega de ojos azules, sorda de nube y rocas.
Nada me diste; sólo la deseada manzana:
un mes de paraíso, cien años de serpiente.

Nada más que el arco iris en su jaula de lluvia
y la rosa que expira en su cruz de perfume.
El mundo entero gime en el yunque otoñal.
El fuego inexorable consume la hojarasca.

Bosque andrajoso, pierdes tus remiendos dorados
por obra del otoño, mal aprendiz de sastre.
Un reloj de corteza mide el tiempo del árbol.
El mirlo anuncia el juicio final de las hormigas.

Ablanda, forjador otoñal, en el yunque
mi corazón forjado del metal del olvido.
Dale una oscura forma de escarcela de lágrimas.
A cada golpe tiembla un nido de palomas.

A cada golpe tiembla mi corazón atado
a su yunque en la última hoguera de la tarde.
Las brasas esparcidas arden en las vantanas.
Sobre mi frente el tiempo avienta las cenizas.

Blacksmith of autumn, forge my heart,
Give shape to its cluster upon your golden anvil.
At each blow the metal of forgetfulness moans;
With the breath of the bellows, even the clouds burn.

I am a man dressed in dry leaves;
My breast harbors liquids from exhausted fountains.
The talking bird of former times once sang:
The world is yours. Take it. Light brands your forehead.

I shouted my love to you, dauntless nature,
Blind and blue-eyed, deaf with rocks and clouds.
You said nothing to me. Only the longed-for apple:
A month of paradise, a hundred years of serpent.

Nothing but the rainbow in its cage of raindrops
And the rose expiring on its cross of perfume,
The whole world moans on the autumnal anvil,
And inexorable fire consuming shriveled foliage.

Tattered forest, you are losing your golden patches;
This is autumn's doing, unskillful tailor's apprentice.
A clock made of bark measures out the tree's lifetime
And the thrush announces the last judgement of ants.

Autumnal blacksmith, temper my heart on the anvil,
My heart forged from the metal of foregetfulness,
Give it the dark shape of a pouch filled with tears,
At each hammerblow a dove's nest trembles.

At each blow my heart trembles,
Asttached to its anvil in the last hearthfire of twilight.
A sprinkling of embers still glows through the windows,
Over my forehead time scatters the ashes.

EL CONDENADO

Yo no sembré la planta del espino,
roedor de jardines.
No puse en libertad a ese puma de llamas
que devora furioso las columnas.

¡Os juro! No soy yo
el hombre que destruye los cereales.
No soy el inventor
del ocaso de sangre.

Yo no soy yo.
No conduzcáis mi sombra sobre el muro.
No merezco la siembra de plomo de la muerte,
yo, sembrador de vida,
que os amo tanto, verdugos inocentes,
al mismo tiempo víctimas,
puesto que soy la parte más noble de vosotros.

I did not sow that spiny weed
That gnaws at gardens.
I did not free that puma of flames,
Furious devourer of columns.

I swear to you! I am not a man
Who destroys grainfields.
I did not create
The bleeding sunset.

I am not the one.
Do not drive my shadow up to the wall;
I do not merit the leaden seed of death,
I, seedsman of life,
I who loved you, innocent excutioners,
Victims at the same time,
Seeing that I am the noblest part of you.

HOMBRE PLANETARIO

"Vivimos en el fondo de un gran Océano de aire."
(Los sabios geofísicos)

I

Salgo a la calle como cada día.
Fantasma entre las casas me pregunto
el color de la hora, el rostro incierto
del azul que me mira
hasta arder en su fuego más recóndito.
La ciudad me cautiva, red de piedra.
Las calles se persiguen,
se congregan en torno
de las plazas de sol, grandes tambores
forrados con la piel
de cordero del cielo.
¿Soy ese hombre que mira desde el puente
los relumbres del río,
vitrina de las nubes?
Fui Ulises, Parsifal,
Hamlet y Segismundo y muchos otros
antes de ser el personaje adusto
con un gabán de viento que atraviesa
el teatro de la calle.

II

Camino, mas no avanzo.
Mis pasos me conducen a la nada
por una calle, tumba de hojas secas
o sucesión de puertas condenadas.
¿Soy esa sombra sola
que aparece de pronto sobre el vidrio
de los escaparates?
¿O aquel hombre que pasa

PLANETARY MAN

We live in the depths of a great ocean of air.
(Geophysical Scientists)

I

I go out into the street every day
Like a shadow among houses I ask myself
The color of the hour, the doubtful face
Of the blue that stares at me
Until it burns in its most secret fire.
The city captures me, net of stone.
The streets pursue me,
Congregating all about
The plazas of the sun, great furry drums
Made of the sheepskin
Of the sky.
Am I this man who from the bridge
Stares down at the glitter of the river,
Showcase of clouds?
I was Ulysses, Parsifal,
Hamlet and Sigismundo and many others
Before being the solemn person
In a raincoat of wind who crosses
The stage of the street.

II

I walk but I do not advance.
My footsteps lead nowhere
Through a street, a tomb of dry leaves,
Or a succession of condemned doorways.
Am I this single shadow
Which suddenly appears in the glass
Of the shopwindows?
Or that man who goes by

y que entra siempre por la misma puerta?
Me reconozco en todos, pero nunca
me encuentro en donde estoy. No voy conmigo
sino muy pocas veces, a escondidas.
Me busco casi siempre sin hallarme,
y mis monedas cuento a medianoche.
¿Malbaraté el caudal de mi existencia?
¿Dilapidé mi oro? Nada importa:
se pasa sin pagar al fin del viaje
la invisible frontera.

III

Lunes, puntual obrero, me visitas
con tu faz de domingo ya difunto,
pero en verdad más martes que otro día.
El mièrcoles y el jueves son gemelos
perdidos en el fondo de ese túnel
con un rumor de ruedas y vajilla,
con pasos y con lluvia
que conduce hasta el viernes, puerta falsa
por donde llega el sábado,
cómplice disfrazado de domingo,
inspector de las cuentas semanales
y también de caminos y jardines,
siempre dispuesto a levantarse tarde,
a recoger el sol sobre una silla
y a cerrar una puerta hacia el pasado.

IV

¿Soy sólo un rostro, un nombre
un mecanismo oscuro y misterioso
que responde a la planta y al lucero?
Yo sé que este armatoste de cal viva

And who always enters the same doorway?
I recognize myself in every one, but never
Meet myself where I am. I do not accompany myself
Or very rarely, secretly.
I seek nearly always without finding myself,
And my coins I count at midnight.
Have I squandered the riches of my existence?
Have I wasted my gold? It doesn't matter:
The end of the trip is reached free of charge,
The invisible frontier.

III

Monday, punctual worker, you visit me
With your Sunday face already dead,
But really more Tuesday than any other day.
Wednesday and Thursday are twins,
Lost in the depths of this tunnel
With a murmur of wheels and knives and forks,
With steps and rain
Which lead to Friday, false door
Through which Saturday arrives,
Disguised accomplice of Sunday,
Inspector of weekly accounts,
And also roads and gardens,
Always inclined to get up late,
To collect sun on a chair
And close a door toward the past.

IV

Am I merely a face, a name
An obscure and mysterious mechanism
Which responds to the plant and the evening star?
I know that this hulk of living calcium

con ropaje de polvo
que marca mi presencia entre los hombres
me acompaña de paso, ya que un día
irá a habitar vacío
de mi bajo la tierra.
¿Qué mueve el mecanismo transitorio?
Soy sólo un visitante
y creo ser el dueño de casa de mi cuerpo,
nocturna madriguera iluminada
por un fulgor eterno.

V

Eternidad, te busco en cada cosa:
en la piedra quemada por los siglos,
en el árbol que muere y que renace,
en el río que corre
sin volver atrás nunca.
Eternidad, te busco en el espacio,
en el cielo nocturno donde boga
el luminoso enjambre,
en el alba que vuelve
todos los días a la misma hora.
Eternidad, te busco en el minuto
disfrazado de pájaro,
pero que es gota de agua
que cae y se renueva
sin agotarse nunca.
Eternidad, tus signos me rodean,
mas yo soy transitorio:
un simple pasajero del planeta.

In raiments of dust
Which indicates my presence among men
Temporarily accompanies me, until one day
It will go to live under ground
Empty of me.
What moves the transitory mechanism?
I am only a visitor
Believing I am the master of the house of my body,
Burrow of night, lit by
An eternal brightness.

V

Eternity I seek you in everything:
In the stone burned by centuries,
In the tree which dies and is reborn,
In the river that flows onward
Never to return.
Eternity I seek you in space,
Where the luminous swarm
Curves over the night sky
And in the dawn which returns
Every day at the same hour.
Eternity, I seek you in the moment,
Disguised as a bird,
But which is a drop of water
Which falls and is renewed,
Inexhaustibly.
Eternity, your signs surround me,
But I am transitory:
A simple passenger on the planet.

VI

Tiempo cósmico, reinas
sin fin omnipresente,
pulpo gris
sin ayer ni mañana, siempre ahora,
dormido en el espacio.
Tu masa no se mide por minutos,
por horas o por días.
No eres el caracol
enrollado, cautivo
en el reloj del hombre.
Yo te mido mejor, oh inmensurable,
por amarguras o por alegrias
y por silencios o por soledades
de sesenta suspiros cada una.
Yo viví sesenta años en un día
y en una hora de amor
sesenta eternidades.

VII

Amor es más que la sabiduría:
es la resurrección, vida segunda.
El ser que ama revive
o vive doblemente.
El amor es resumen de la tierra,
es luz, música, sueño
y fruta material
que gustamos con todos los sentidos.
¡Oh mujer que penetras en mis venas
como el cielo en los ríos!
Tu cuerpo es un país de leche y miel
que recorro sediento
Me abrevo en tu semblante de agua fresca,

VI

Cosmic time, you reign
Endlessly everywhere,
Grey octopus
Without yesterday or to-morrow, always now,
Sleeping in space.
Your mass is not measured in minutes
Hours or days.
You are not the whorled snail
Captive
In a man's watch.
I measure you better, oh immeasurable,
In bitterness or joy
And by silences or solitudes,
Sixty sighs to each.
I have lived sixty years in a day
And sixty eternities
In an hour of love.

VII

Love is more than wisdom:
It is the resurrection, a second life.
The being who loves lives again,
Or lives twice.
Love is the summation of the earth,
It is light, music, sleep,
The material fruit
Which we enjoy with all the senses.
Oh woman you who penetrate my veins
As the sky does rivers!
Your body is a land of milk and honey
I thirstily traverse.
In your face, pure as water,

de arroyo primigenio
en mi jornada ardiente hacia el origen
del manantial perdido.
Minero del amor, cavo sin tregua
hasta hallar el filón del infinito.

VIII

Eva en el Siglo Veinte va calzada
de cuero de la sierpe fabulosa
y viste cada día
de un color diferente.
Acude al paraíso en automóvil,
mas no puede ocultar bajo la máscara
su identidad celeste.
Aprende los oficios de los hombres.
Cuida su corazón en una jaula
con flores, hijos, pájaros.
Imprime en vacaciones
la forma de su cuerpo
en la grama o la arena.
En su bolso de espejos
con el leve pañuelo de heliotropo
guarda las llaves de las siete puertas
del paraíso humano,
paraíso privado con teléfono,
máquina de lavar hojas de parra,
televisión azul como la luna
y refrigeradora con manzanas.

IX

Hombres, mujeres jóvenes,
dentro de una vitrina
con adornos de plantas,

I quench my thirst from a primordial spring,
In my day's travel toward the origin
Of the lost freshet of rain.
Miner of love, I dig ceaselessly
Till I find the vein of the infinite.

VIII

In the Twentieth Century, Eve goes
Shod in fabulous snakeskin
And dresses in a different color
Every day.
She sets out for the Garden of Eden
In an automobile but can not hide,
Her celestial identity, beneath her mask.
She learns the occupations of men.
She tends her heart in a cage
Of flowers, children, birds.
During vacations she imprints
The shape of her body
On the grass or the sand.
In her mirrored purse
With the delicate heliotrope handkerchief
She keeps the keys to the seven doors
Of an earthly Paradise,
A private paradise with a telephone,
A machine for washing grapeleaves
Television blue as the moon
And refrigerators full of apples.

IX

Men, young women,
Sit smiling
Behind a plate glass

se sientan y sonríen,
se miran, examinan sus vestidos,
cambian palabras de humo,
saborean el tiempo en rebanadas
o por cucharaditas deleitosas.
Deshojan un bostezo entre los dedos.
Un arbusto de caucho aspira el humo
y se cree en el trópico.
Inadvertido, entra en la vitrina
el poniente vestido de amarillo.
Salid, hombres, mujeres, a la calle:
sobre el asfalto expira una paloma
atropellada por un automóvil.

X

Mienten Juan el Obeso, José el Calvo,
Francisco el Tartamudo,
mienten el flaco, el grande, mienten todos,
hablan con dulce voz, siempre sonríen
mientras arman sus redes en la sombra
para atrapar su víctima
por algunas monedas.
La amistad, el amor, el cielo mismo
falsificado en píldoras
pesan en su balanza fraudulenta
para ganar, multiplicar sus bienes
y ser los potentados de este mundo,
fantasmas que recorren sus palacios
de salones inmensos con alfombras
y retratos al óleo
en donde la humedad vierte su lágrima.

Decorated with plants;
They look at each other, pass on each other's cloths
Exchange words of smoke,
Relishing time in slices
Or delicious spoonfuls.
They strip the petals from a yawn with their fingers.
A rubber tree breathes the smoke
And fancies itself in the tropics,
Accidentally the sunset, dressed in yellow,
Enters through the plate glass.
Go forth, men and women into the street:
On the pavement a dove is dying
Run over by an automobile.

X

Juan the Fat and José the Bald
Francisco the Stutterer are lying,
The thin, the tall, they're all lying;
They speak with soft voices, always smiling
While they prepare their nets in the dark
To trap their victims
For a certain amount of money.
Friendship, love, even heaven
Counterfeited in pills
They weigh in their deceitful scales
To make money, multiply their property
And become the potentates of this worlds,
Shadows who traverse their palaces
With huge salons and deep rugs
And oil paintings
Where moisture sheds a tear.

XI

Loor a Mister Huntington — filántropo
nacido en el país de las manzanas,
las antiguas Misiones coloniales
y las rojas ardillas —
que legó su fortuna
para que los granjeros de su pueblo
pudieran admirar los manuscritos
de Cabeza de Vaca, navegante,
descubridor de Texas,
señor del cacto y de la arena cálida.
Contra las pobres flechas de los indios
luchó con su arcabuz y su armadura
y lanzó su caballo de batalla
contra los pies desnudos.
Conquistador de polvo: yo bendigo
al pueblo de las flechas.

XII

Gloria a los fabricantes de automóviles
que han poblado el planeta
de rodantes alcobas,
salones, catafalcos
a plazos, camarines de amuletos
y flores, donde viaja
la vanidad inflada de sus dueños,
¡oh amos de la prisa, los que arrancan
de su sueño a los árboles!
Gloria a los inventores
de la Gran Vitamina Universal
para aliviar los males de la tierra.
(¿Qué haré yo sin mi augustia metafísica,
sin mi dolencia azul? ¿Qué harán los hombres

XI

Praised be Mister Huntington — philantropist
Born in the country of apples,
Of ancient colonial missions
With red squirrels,
Who left his fortune
So that the farmers of his town
Could admire the manuscripts
Of Cabeza la Vaca, navigator,
Discoverer of Texas,
Lord of the cactus and the hot sand.
Against the poor arrows of the Indians
He fought with crossbow and armor
And flung his warhorses
Against their naked feet.
Conqueror of dust: I bless
The people of the arrows.

XII

Hail to the manufacturers of automobiles
Who have populated the planet
With rolling bedrooms,
Salons, catafalques
On installment, closets of amulets
And flowers in which the inflated vanity
Of their owners travels about,
Oh masters of speed, who snatch
The trees from their sleep!
Hail to the inventors
Of the Great Universal Vitamin
To alleviate the evils of the earth.
(What should I do without my metaphysical anguish
My blue suffering? What shall men do

151

cuando ya nada sientan, mecanismos
perfectos, uniformes?)

XIII

¿Los artefactos, las perfectas máquinas,
el autómata de ojo de luz verde
igualan por lo menos a una abeja
dotada de reflejos naturales,
que conoce el secreto
del mundo de las plantas
y se dirige sola en el espacio
a buscar material entre las flores
para su azucarada, sutil fábrica?
Todo puede crear la humana ciencia,
menos ese resorte del instinto
o de la voluntad, menos la vida.
Inventor de las máquinas volantes
quiere el hombre viajar hacia los astros,
crear nuevos satélites celestes
y disparar cohetes a la luna
sin haber descifrado el gran enigma
del oscuro planeta en que vivimos.
Yo intento comprender los movimientos
de plantas y animales y me digo:
Por ahora me basta con la tierra.

XIV

¡Escuchad cómo estallan las corolas!
La abeja celestina
les entrega mensajes fecundantes.
Los vegetales reptan enlazados,
se alzan hacia la luz
con idéntica augustia

When they finally feel nothing, perfect
Mechanisms in uniform?)

XIII

The artefacts, the perfect machines,
The automaton with the eye of green light
Do they even match a bee
Endowed with natural reflexes
Which knows the secret
Of the world of planets
And only takes off into space
To seek among the flowers for the sources
Of its sweetening, subtle refinery?
Human science can create everything,
Except for this device of instinct
Or of will, except for life.
Inventor of machines that fly,
Man wants to voyage to the stars,
Create new satellites in space
And shoot rockets at the moon
Without having deciphered the great enigma
Of the obscure planet on which we dwell.
I, eager to know the movements
Of plants and animals, say to myself:
At present earth is enough for me.

XIV

Hear how the corollas burst open!
The bee, a procuress,
Bears fecundating messages to them
The plants writhing enlaced
Rise to the light
With identical longing to enjoy

a extasiarse en el reino de los pájaros.
Picos y alas protegen las semillas
del asalto mortal de los insectos.
Y la vida perdura
desde la nube al fondo de los mares
en donde el pez humilde,
hermano mutilado,
pordiosero del agua,
agita sus harapos.
Seres elementales, plantas, piedras,
animallilos libres y perfectos:
fragmentos nada más del puro cántico
total del universo.

XV

¿Dónde se encuentra, rosa,
tu máquina secreta
que te forma y te enciende, brasa viva
del carbón de la sombra
y te impulsa a lo alto
a expresar en carmín y terciopelo
tu gozo de vivir sobre la tierra?
¿Qué oculto motor verde,
qué eje te redondea, fuego cóncavo,
breve nido de llamas?
¿Qué vienes a decir con tantos labios?
¿Eres sólo una boca del misterio
que intenta pronunciar una palabra
nunca oída hasta ahora
para cambiar el curso de este mundo?
¿O eres acaso el beso de la tierra
a todo lo que vive,
prueba de amor de un día
a las cosas oscuras
devoradas a medias por la muerte?

Ecstasy in the kingdom of the birds.
Spines and wings protect the seeds
From the deadly assault of insects.
And life goes on
Where the humble fish,
A mutilated brother,
Almoner of water,
Waves its rags.
Elemental beings, plants, stones,
Tiny beasts, perfect and free;
None other than fragments of the pure
And total song of the universe.

XV

Where can we find, rose,
Your secret mechanism
Which forms and sets you aflame, live ember
From coals of shadows,
and pushes you to the heights
To express your joy at living on earth
In carmine and velvet?
What hidden green motor,
What lathe rounded you, concave fire,
Brief nest of flames?
What do you come to say with so many lips?
Are you only a mysterious mouth
About to pronounce a word
Never heard before
Which will change the destiny of the world?
Or are you perhaps the earth's kiss
For all that lives,
Proof of one day's love
For dark things
Half devoured by death?

XVI

Soy hombre, mineral y planta a un tiempo,
relieve del planeta, pez del aire,
un ser terrestre en suma.
Arbol del Amazonas mis arterias,
mi frente de París, ojos del trópico,
mi lengua americana y española,
hombros de Nueva York y de Moscú,
pero fija, invisible,
mi raíz en el suelo equinoccial,
nutriéndose del agua de los ríos
y de la sangre verde que circula
por el frágil, alado cuerpecillo
del loro, profesor de ortología,
del saltamontes y del colibrí,
mis ínfimos aliados naturales.

XVII

¡Oh fábula moderna!: los soldados
de plomo de los cuentos infantiles
cobran vida, se animan
y crecen, crecen, crecen
hasta llegar a ser de más tamaño
que los hombres. Intentan
disparar con sus manos el relámpago
para encerrar el alba en una cárcel,
descolgar las estrellas
para adornar sus hombros
y acudir al banquete de la noche.
Invaden por millares los jardines,
y con oscuras máquinas de muerte
exterminan el verde de este mundo
cubriéndolo de ruinas,

XVI

I am man, mineral and plant at the same time,
A hump on the planet, a fish of air,
In short, a terrestrial being.
My arteries, an Amazonian tree.
My forehead of Paris, eyes tropical.
My tongue American and Spanish
Shoulders of New York and of Moscow.
But my root invisibly fixed
In the equinoxial soil,
Nourished by the water of the rivers
And the green blood that circulates
Through the fragile, winged little body
Of the parrot, professor of grammar,
Of grasshoppers and of the hummingbird,
My smallest natural allies.

XVII

Oh modern Fable: lead soldiers
Out of stories for children
Come to life, animated,
And grow, grow, grow
Until they become larger
Than men! They endeavor
To fire off the lighting with their hands,
To imprison dawn in a cell,
Take down the stars
To decorate their shoulders
And attend the banquet of night.
By thousands they invade gardens
And with obscure machines for murder
They exterminate the green of this world
Covering it with ruins,

de víctimas o estatuas
en mangas de camisa.

XVIII

Juan Cordero, varón de miel oscura,
pecho de cuero, entraña enternecida,
capitán de los surcos
y maestro de escuela de los pájaros,
yaces sin vida cerca de tu casa,
como un saco de paja y de ceniza,
un saco agujereado
que el rocío humedece con sus lágrimas.
¿Qué crimen cometiste? Solo un grito:
"¡Vivan los pueblos libres!" Los soldados
dispararon sus armas
sobre ti, Juan Cordero, y tus hermanos,
incendiaron las trojes
y arrascaron la tierra de tus padres.
(Dios estaba escondido en una granja
y contempló en silencio
el sacrificio de los inocentes
y su mundo en escombros.)

XIX

Vendrá un dia más puro que los otros:
estallará la paz sobre la tierra
como un sol de cristal. Un fulgor nuevo
envolverá las cosas.
Los hombres cantarán en los caminos,
libres ya de la muerte solapada.
El trigo crecerá sobre los restos
de las armas destruídas
y nadie verterá

With victims or statues
In shirtsleeves.

XVIII

John Everyman, dark honey-colored male,
Chest of leather, with bowels of pity,
Captain of the furrows
And schoolmaster to the birds,
You lie near your house, lifeless,
Like a sack of ashes and straw,
A sack full of holes
Wet with the tears of the dew.
What crime did you commit? Only to cry:
"Long live the free peoples!" Soldiers
Fired their guns at you,
John Everyman, and at your brothers,
Set fire to the granaries
And laid waste the fields of your fathers.
(God was hidden in a farmhouse
And watched in silence
The sacrifice of the innocents
And his world turned to rubble.)

XIX

There will come a day purer than ever before:
Peace will burst out over the earth
Like a crystal sun. Everything
Will shine with a new brilliance.
Men will sing on the highways,
Free now of artful death.
Wheat will grow over the remains
Of demolished weapons
And no one will shed

la sangre de su hermano.
El mundo será entonces de las fuentes
y las espigas, que impondrán su imperio
de abundancia y frescura sin fronteras.
Los ancianos tan sólo, en el domingo
de su vida apacible,
esperarán la muerte,
la muerte natural, fin de jornada,
paisaje más hermoso que el poniente.

XX

Yo soy el habitante de las piedras
sin memoria, con sed de sombra verde;
yo soy el ciudadano de cien pueblos
y de las prodigiosas Capitales,
el Hombre Planetario,
tripulante de todas las ventanas
de la Tierra aturdida de motores.
Soy el hombre de Tokio, que se nutre
de bambú y pececillos;
el minero de Europa,
hermano de la noche;
el labrador del Congo y de la arena,
el pescador de ostiones polinesios,
soy el indio de América, el mestizo,
el amarillo, el negro
y soy los demás hombres del planeta.
Sobre mi corazón firman los pueblos
un tratado de paz hasta la muerte.

The blood of his brother.
There will be a world then of wheatears
And fountains, imposing its limitless domination
Of flourishing abundance.
The aged, so lonely in the Sunday,
Of their peaceful lives,
Shall wait for death,
A natural death, the end of the day,
A landscape fairer than that of the sunset.

XX

I am the dweller in stones
Without memory, thirsty for green shadow;
I am the citizen of a hundred towns
And the prodigious Capitals,
The Planetary Man,
Crewman of all the windows
Of Earth, giddy with motors
Iam the man of Tokio, nourished
On bamboo and little fish;
The European miner,
Brother of night;
The Congo farmer, the worker in the sand,
The fisherman of Polynesian oysters,
I am the Indian of America, the mestizo,
The yellow, the black,
And I am all other men of the planet.
Upon my heart the peoples
Sign a treaty of peace until death.

LOS TERRÍCOLAS

Os digo: nuestro siglo es fabuloso,
Crepúsculo del Hombre
sitiado por millares de terrícolas
sin ojos para ver nubes o flores,
sólo nutridos de oro,
incapaces de oír la música del mundo,
aprendices o larvas del Autómata próximo.

Terrícolas que entierran las estatuas,
emparedan los libros,
echan al mar las llaves del planeta,
desconocen el lirio,
todo ponen en venta, hasta el claro de luna;
proclaman el mundial degüello de los cisnes
como materia prima para una nueva industria.

Terrícolas iguales en su gesto y ropaje
y por dentro vacíos,
negadores del sol, seres de sombra,
falanges del bostezo y del olvido,
sublevación inmensa
contra el Hombre y su mundo de amor y maravilla
para instaurar el reino de las Palabras Huecas.

El reino de los cielos con máquinas volantes,
el reino de la músicas mecánicas
y las Casas Idénticas
—desmesuradas tumbas con pisos y ventanas—,
el Reino Sordomudo,
obediente a señales y cifras luminosas,
palpitantes avispas de los muros.

THE TERRESTRIANS

I tell you: ours is a fabulous century,
The twilight of Man
Besieged by thousands of terrestrians
Without eyes to see clouds or flowers,
Nourished on gold alone,
Incapable of hearing the music of the world,
Apprentices or larvae of the coming Automatom.

Terrestrians who bury statues
And wall up books,
Throw the keys of the planet into the sea,
They never heard of lillies,
They sell anything, even moonlight;
They proclaim a worldwide cutting of swans throats
To provide the basic material for a new industry.

Terrestrians all alike in dress and movement,
And within hollow,
Deniers of sun, creatures of shadow,
Phalanxes of the yawn and forgetfulness,
Immense uprising
Against Man and his world of love and marvels
To install the kingdom of Empty Words.

The kingdom of skies full of flying machines,
The kingdom of mechanical music
And Identical Houses
— Numberless tombs with floors and windows —
The Deaf and Dumb Kingdom,
Which obeys signs and luminous numbers,
Palpitating wasps in the walls.

No existen manantiales
en la Ciudad Terrícola.
En moradas de vidrio
la sed eterna habita.
La sed huye en torrentes de automóviles
hacia constelaciones de neón, y regresa
en su ronda mortal de insectos de colores.

¡Oh siglo fabuloso!
El planeta contempla la agonía
de los últimos hombres
acosados sin fin por los terrícolas
dinámicos, idénticos,
que avanzan sepultando los cuadros y los libros,
fortaleza final de los humanos sueños.

There are no springs
In the Terrestrial City.
Eternal thirst
Lives in glass dwellings.
Thirst flees in torrents of automobiles
Toward neon constellations, and returns again
In a vicious circle of colored insects.

Of fabulous century!
The planet contemplates the agony
Of the last men
Endlessly pursued by the terrestrians.
Identical and dynamic,
Advancing as they bury pictures and books,
The last fortress of human dreams.

TEORÍA DEL GUACAMAYO

Maravilla del Nuevo Mundo,
la gran brasa con alas,
reducido crepúsculo volante,
alumbra con su luz las hojas verdes.

Todo es fulgor,
promesa o paraíso,
carnal deslumbramiento,
certidumbre del sol en los colores,
vestidura vistosa de lo real.

El ojo se complace en sus facetas,
espejismo aleteante del deseo,
ráfaga del calor hecha pintura,
dios estival doméstico.

Huésped del árbol y de la morada,
sapiente guacamayo,
con silabario vegetal afirmas
tu alianza con el mundo de los hombres,
la alegría fraterna
del Trópico en su ambiente de familia.

El guacamayo y el sol
recomienzan su diálogo amarillo.
El ala responde al reflejo
con la elocuencia minuciosa de sus plumas
en llamas superpuestas
al oro sucesivo.

Imagen del ardor,
gloria que emprende el vuelo
para disimularse entre las ramas
con disfraz de gran fruto.

THEORY OF THE MACAW

Marvel of the new world,
Live coal with wings,
Miniature flying sunset,
Illuminating the green leaves with its light.

All is brightness,
Promise or paradise,
Fleshly dazzle of brilliance,
Multicolored certainty of sun,
Garish garment of reality.

The eye delights in its facets,
Palpitating illusion of desire,
Scrap of heat turned into painting,
Domestic god of summer.

Guest of the tree and the dwelling,
Wise macaw,
With your leafy primer you affirm
Your alliance with the world of men,
The gay fraternity
Of the Tropics, with its feeling of family.

The macaw and the sun
Renew their yellow dialog.
The wing responds to the reflection
With the tiny eloquence of its feathers
In flames superimposed
Over layers of gold.

The image of ardor,
Glory which takes flight
To hide itself in the branches
In the guise of a great fruit.

Ave roja triunfante,
claridad del trópico:
imprime tu figura
sobre el códice
de mi pecho aborigen.

El floripondio y el guacamayo
protegen mi sueño
de hombre de América
mientras las plantas crecen
en pocas horas
restableciendo la selva
en la Ciudad Fértil.

Copa del sueño, floripondio,
heraldo del color, guacamayo:
signos de un reino silvestre
gobernado por las alas
de la Dinastía Verde del Trópico.

Oh pájaro escapado de una mina de esmeraldas
y de una cueva de oro,
guacamayo amigo,
émulo de las flores
en tus plumas vuela
el tesoro de Atahualpa.

Ave sagrada de las tribus,
testigo prehistórico
relatas la crónica del Descubrimento
y la diaria aventura
de los nuevos conquistadores,
nosotros hijos de los hijos.
— ¿Quién no guarda escondida
la armadura de huesos
para las conquista del reino de la sombra? —

Triumphant red bird
Tropical peal of bells,
Print your image
Upon the codex
Of my native breast.

The floripondio and the macaw
Protect my dream
As American man
While plants
Grow in a few hours
Reinstating the forest
In the fertile City.

Floripondio, cup of dreams,
Macaw, herald of color:
Insignia of a sylvan kingdom,
Governed by the wings
Of the Green Dynasty of the Tropics.

O bird, escaped from an emerald mine
And a cave of gold,
Friend Macaw,
Emulating the flowers:
The treasure of Atahualpa
Flies in your feathers.

Sacred bird of the native tribes,
Prehistoric witness:
You relate the chronicle of the discovery
And the daily adventure
Of the new conquistadors,
We, the sons of their sons —
Who does not keep hidden
That bony armor
For the conquest of the kingdom of darkness? —

Ave de la Utopía:
Tu ojo soñoliento
y voz fingida
me muestran las señales en las plantas y rocas
que guían a las Islas del Eterno Domingo.
Yo desgrano el maíz dorado de mis días
en el cántaro oscuro de la edad
y me preparo
para el más prodigioso de los viajes.

Utopian bird:
Your sleepy eye
And dissembling voice
Reveal to me the signals in plants and stones
Which lead to the Isles of Eternal Sunday.
I shell the golden corn of my days
Into the dark jar of age
And prepare myself
For the most prodigious journey of all.

OCASO DE ATAHUALPA

Imperio de los hombres hermanos de los riscos,
amigos del torrente,
fundadores de pueblos
en la región más alta del volcán y la nube,
¡oh padres cariñosos del surco y la semilla!:
nada pueden los verdes escuadrones
del maíz contra el pecho violento del caballo
ganando a la carrera
la vastedad del suelo predilecto del sol.

¿Qué puede la vistosa plumería
ceremonial contra los arcabuces?
Guacamayo imperial Atahualpa,
acudes a la cita
seguido por millares de súbditos sin armas,
en hileras de fiesta,
susurrantes de sílabas humildes y sandalias.

Plaza de Cajamarca, jaula inmensa
de la Muerte Emplumada.
Hecatombe de pájaros,
combate de las alas
contra el casco implacable del caballo.
Los caciques se doblan, águilas moribundas.
No puede el griterío
detener el relámpago.
Mueren los alfareros,
mueren los tejedores,
mueren los compañeros de la sacra vicuña,
mueren los amadores de la tierra y los astros.
Nunca viera el sol indio tanta sangre.

DEATH OF ATAHUALPA

Empire of men, brothers to the mountain peaks
Friends of the torrent,
Founders of villages
In the highest region of the volcano and the cloud,
Oh tender fathers of the furrow and the seed!
The green squadrons of the corn
Can do nothing against the violent charger's breast
Winning at a charge
The vastness of the sunloved soil.

What can the gaudy ceremonial plumage
Achieve against crossbows?
Atahualpa, the imperial macaw,
You go to the tryst
Followed by thousands of unarmed subjects,
In formations for a fiesta
A whispering of sandals and soft speech.

Plaza de Cajamarca, immese cage
Of Plumed Death,
Hetacomb of birds,
Combat of wings
Against the implacable charger's hoof,
The caciques sink down, dying eagles.
Shouting can not
Turn aside the lightning.
The potters die,
The weavers die,
The companions of the sacred vicuña die,
The lovers of earth and sky perish.
Never shall the Indian sun see so much blood.

Atahualpa: desciende de tus andas de oro.
Aquí está tu collar de esmeraldas
en la mano sangrienta del caudillo de hierro.
El día muere sobre tantas vidas,
la noche cae sobre tantas muertes.

El dios sol ha dejado que se cumpla el destino.
En la flauta de hueso de una tibia
Llora el fin de su pueblo
Quilliscacha, escondido
tras de un peñasco de la Cordillera.

Atahualpa repite su derrota
herido cuantas veces en mi pecho
por un Pizarro íntimo.
Vencedor y vencido luchan en mi interior:
el rey indio despliega su plumaje,
el agua de los siglos lava el suelo
que cubren las sonrisas del maíz
y el jinete de hierro se arrodilla.

Atahualpa: descend from your golden litter.
Here is your emerald necklace
In the bloody hand of the iron chieftain.
Day dies above so many lives,
Night falls over so many dead.

The sun god has allowed destiny to be fulfilled.
Hidden behind a peak of the Gordilleras,
Quilliscacha laments
With the flute of a shinbone,
The end of his people.

Atahualpa repeats his overthrow
With countless wounds in my breast
Given by an intimate Pizzaro.
Victor and vanquished
Struggle within me:
The Indian king spreads his plumage,
The water of centuries waters the soil
Covered with the smiles of maize
And the iron horseman kneels.

LOS ANTEPASADOS

Tumbe, Quitumbe, Guayanay,
adoradores del Idolo de Piedra Verde,
jefes remotos consultores de los astros,
capitanes del mar,
constructores de moradas sobre los árboles:
Os venero
y rindo culto,
golpeando las palmas de mis manos
en dirección del sol.

Tumbe, amigo de las iguanas;
Quitumbe, explorador
de la Tierra de los Colibríes;
Guayanay, protegido de los cóndores,
descubridor de la Isla Desierta
y la Isla del Pelícano Sagrado
portador de los peces:
Traedme la Gran Mazorca de Oro
hermana del guacamayo,
la Mazorca de maíz inagotable
para alimento de mi pueblo.

Tumbe, Quitumbe, Guayanay:
hombres de paz vestidos con la cota
de plumas de colores,
astrónomos ¡oh padres!
señaladme el camino
de la floresta antigua
donde el Gran Guacamayo divulga su secreto
en una lengua extraña
olvidada hace siglos.

Tumbe, Quitumbe, Guayanay;
Adorers of the Idol of Green Stone,
Remote chiefs consultors of stars,
Captains of the sea,
Builders of dwellings above the tree:
I venerate you
And I worship
Clapping the palms of my hands
In the direction of the sun.

Tumbe, friend of the iguanas;
Quitumbe explorer
Of the Land of the Hummingbirds;
Guayanay, protector of condors,
Discoverer of the Desert Island
And the Island of the Sacred Pelican,
Bearer of fish:
Fetch me the great Ear of Gold,
Sister of the macaw,
The Ear of inexhaustible maize
To feed my people.

Tumbe, Quitumbe, Guayanay;
Men of peace dressed in armor
Of colored feathers,
Astronomers, oh fathers!
Point out the way to
The ancient blooming forest
Where the Great Macaw divulges his secret
In a strange language
Forgotten for centuries.

CRONICA DE LAS INDIAS
1965

EL PACIFICADOR

Argumento del poema

En el siglo XVI, el conquistador Gonzalo Pizarro se rebeló contra las Ordenanzas y Leyes de Indias, que favorecían a los aborígenes, y se proclamó "Protector de los Encomenderos". Fue el primer Dictador del Nuevo Mundo. "Desde Quito hasta las fronteras septentrionales de Chile — dice Prescott —, todo el país reconoció la autoridad de Pizarro. Sus tropas estaban bajo un pie excelente... Dícese que los preparativos para la campaña le costaron un millón de pesos de oro." La Corona española envió como pacificador al clérigo Pedro de La Gasca, quien organizó en Panamá una Flota, con la cual invadió los dominios de Pizarro, después de navegar por el Océano Pacífico y escapar de una gran tempestad. El ejército leal atravesó una extensa región por las costas del Ecuador y del Perú y venció a las tropas de Pizarro en Jaquijaguana, casi sin derramamiento de sangre. La fuerza del convencimiento en la justicia de su causa dio la victoria al ejército de La Gasca. Gonzalo Pizarro se rindió y fue decapitado en Lima.

J.C.A.

I

La Expedición Naval

¡Vientos del Nuevo Mundo, inflad, inflad las velas!
El Pacífico encrespa sus leones de espuma.
Rechina el maderamen mojado de relámpagos.
Olas, olas o lomos de cetáceos antiguos
golpean empujando los cascos de las naves.
Nunca viera el Océano Armada más potente,
más airosos velámenes y más audaces proas.
Va el Pacificador en la nave almiranta.

THE PEACEMAKER

ARGUMENT OF THE POEM

In the XVI century the conquistador, Gonzalo Pizarro, rebelled against the Ordinances and Laws of the Indies which favored the natives and proclaimed himself "Protector of the Encomenderos." He was the first Dictator of The New World. "From Quito to the northern frontiers of Chile," says Prescott, "the whole country recognized the authority of Pizarro. His troops were in a state of excellent discipline... It was said that the preparations for the campaign cost him a million gold pesos." The Crown of Spain sent as peacemaker the cleric, Pedro de La Gasca, who, at Panama, organized a fleet with which he invaded Pizarro's dominions, after crossing the Pacific Ocean and escaping a great tempest. The loyalist army traversed a large part of the coast of Ecuador and Peru and defeated Pizarro's troops at Jaquijaguana, almost without shedding blood. The strength of his convictions and the justice of his cause gave the victory to the army of La Gasca. Gonzalo Pizarro surrendered and was decapitated in Lima.

I

THE NAVAL EXPEDITION

Winds of the New World, inflate, inflate the sails!
The Pacific arouses its lions of foam.
The timbers creak, rinsed with lightnings.
Rollers, rollers or backs of ancient whales,
Beat against, drive forward the hulls of the ships.
Never would the ocean see a more potent armada,
More billowy sails and more audacious prows.
The Peacemaker travels in the admiral's flagship.

En vez de la armadura en el cofre labrado
lleva hábitos de clérigo y un legajo de leyes
para el mejor gobierno de los pueblos alzados
por necios Capitanes
adictos a Gonzalo Pizarro, el ambicioso
Gobernador Supremo de esas tierras de América.

La tormenta fosfórica con látigos azules
azota a los galeones que buscan un abrigo
en el desierto gris con pulmones de agua
o montes derrumbándose en abismos de espuma.
Danzan fuegos extraños sobre jarcias y mástiles
—fuegos del otro mundo, según los aterrados
marineros que creen ver arder los navíos
quemados por las ánimas—,
"Son fuegos de San Telmo", dice el sapiente clérigo.
"Luces del infinito, luces son nuestras vidas
que cruzan un instante por la noche del tiempo,
la noche del espacio sideral, fuegos fatuos."

¡Oh fragor de la cúpula inmensa de los cielos
partida por el trueno demoledor y errante!
Batallan los abismos y batallan las nubes
sepultando horizontes en sus tumbas acuáticas.
Implanta la negrura su medroso reinado
de la entraña del pez
al corazón del hombre y al del ave,
transidos de pavor elemental
en la gran noche cósmica.

Doce navíos, doce fortalezas marinas,
orgullosos castillos navegantes,
reciben todo el peso de las líquidas moles
y tratan de escapar a su furia ciclópea.
¡Armada sin ventura
con su jefe postrado de rodillas

Instead of armor from the carved chest,
He wears clerical dress, bears a legacy of laws
For the better rule of peoples, aroused
By foolish captains,
Followers of Gonzalo Pizarro, the ambitious,
Supreme Governor of these American Lands.

The phosphorescent tempest, with its blue whiplash,
Beats the galleons seeking shelter
In the desert, grey with lungs of water,
Or mountains falling into abysses of foam.
Strange fires dance over masts and rigging —
Fires from another world, according to
The panic-stricken sailors who believe the ship is burning,
Set afire by spirits —
"They are the fires of St. Elmo," said the wise Cleric.
Lights from eternity, our lives are lights,
An instant traversing the night of time,
The night of starry space, our light is an ignis fatuus."

Oh, clamor at the great cupola of the heavens,
Split by roving, grinding thunder!
The deeps are battling, the clouds are battling,
Burying horizons in their watery tombs.
Blackness spreads it fearful kingdom
From the guts of fish
To the heart of man and bird,
Shot through with elemental terror
In the great cosmic night.

Twelve ships, twelve marine fortresses,
Arrogant navigating castles
Endure the whole weight of the liquid masses
And seek to escape the cyclopean fury.
Luckless armada
With its chief kneeling

ante una Cruz
en el seno crujiente de una nave en peligro!
¡Proa hacia la Gorgona, fugitivos del mar,
cervatillos dispersos por el Cuerno de Caza
que suena entre las nubes su tocata de muerte!

Isla de la Gorgona, isla diabólica:
¡cuántas fauces de abismo te circundan!
Los canes de las aguas y las piedras
aúllan sin descanso,
ánimas condenadas
defendiendo el acceso
de su infierno de rocas y de espumas.

¡El día, cuánto tarda! !No hay mayor terciopelo
que el de la inmensa noche ecuatorial,
mayor olvido, ilímite soledad sin luceros
en el cielo invadido por la violencia cósmica!
El Pacificador desvelado medita
en la fragilidad de las obras humanas,
amenazadas siempre por designios contrarios;
la soberbia del hombre que lanza un desafío
a las ciegas potencias naturales,
la voluntad que alcanza su victoria
sobre los elementos desatados.
"Morir, morir prefiero,
mas no volver atrás en mi jornada"
—murmura en su monólogo el varón del breviario,
clérigo soñador de la raza de Hamlet
y la de Segismundo.
Su misión es abrir el Libro justiciero,
la ley hacer primar sobre daga y talega
y colgar para siempre la coraza
vieja de la Conquista.

Alba del Nuevo Mundo, por fin tu flor radiante,
abriéndose sin prisa en las alturas,

Before a crucifix
In the creaking bosom of an endangered vessel!
Prow toward Gorgon Island, fugitives of the sea,
Small deer dispersed by The Horn of the Chase
Resounding with blasts of death among the clouds!

Gorgon Island, diabolic island:
How many abysmal jaws surround you!
The hounds of the waters and the rocks
Howl ceaselessly,
Souls condemned
To defend the approaches
To its inferno of cliffs and foam.

The daylight, how late it comes! There's no deeper velvet
Than the immense equatorial darkness,
No deeper oblivion, limitless solitude with never a bright star
In a sky invaded by cosmic violence!
Sleepless, the Peacemaker meditates
On the fragility of human actions,
Menaced continually by contrary designs;
The pride of man who flings a defiance
Against the blind powers of the natural world,
And human will attaining its victory
Over the unleashed force of the elements.
"To die, I would rather die
Than turn back from my journey,"
So the man with the breviary mutters to himself,
Dreaming cleric of the race of Hamlet
And of Sigismundo.
His mission is to open the Book of Justice,
To elevate law supreme over dagger and moneybag
And forever hang up the old
Cuirass of the Conquest.

Dawn of the New World, at last your radiant flower
Opening unhurriedly in the sky

alza bandera blanca en el combate
de mares contra nubes. La calma se establece
y las olas moderan sus balanzas azules
hasta alcanzar el tenso nivel del horizonte.

El Pacificador en la nave almiranta
contempla gravemente el sol ecuatorial,
monarca recubierto de polvillo de oro,
saliendo de las aguas
como en el mito indígena del país de El Dorado.
La Gasca siente el sol del Orbe Nuevo
penetrar en su sangre,
reinar omnipotente sobre seres y cosas,
dios bárbaro al que adoran los hombres naturales
de esos desmantelados paraísos
sonoros de tambores.

De la Gorgona a Manta abre la costa
las verdes perspectivas
del país de los loros y de las esmeraldas,
las tierras fabulosas
de Perruqueta. (Yacen entre leños quemados
los restos de esos pueblos aborígenes,
pescadores, orfebres, alfareros
ataviados de plumas y de telas pintadas,
Señores de las cañas de maíz
y del árbol totémico,
navegantes de Manta en sus balsas veleras
ofreciendo collares y perlas en balanzas,
¡oh civilizaciones inocentes
en su vida pacífica,
aniquiladas fueron por el rayo terrestre
disparado por hombres de coraza y de yelmo
que amaban a su prójimo,
pero no a esos extraños habitantes
que cubrían su cuerpo con plumas de colores
en lugar de armaduras como los caballeros!)

Raises the white flag in the combat
Between sea and clouds. Calm returning,
The rollers smooth out their blue cradles
Level with the taut line of the horizon.

The Peacemaker in the admiral's flagship
Gravely observes the equatorial sun,
A Monarch all powdered with golden dust,
Emerging from the waters
As in the native myth of the land of El Dorado.
La Gasca feels the New Hemisphere's sun
Penetrate his blood,
Reigning over beings and objects,
A barbaric god worshipped by the aboriginal men
Of these ruined paradises,
Sonorous with drums.

From Gorgon Island to Manta the coastline opens
Into green perspectives
Of a country of parrots and emeralds,
The fabulous lands
Of Perruqueta. (Situated between burnt out woods
Are the remains of these Indian peoples,
Fishermen, goldsmiths, makers of pottery,
Decked with feathers and painted weavings,
Lords of the cornstalk
And the totemic tree,
Mariners of Manta in sailing balsas,
Offering necklaces and pearls in trays.
Oh innocent civilizations,
Their peaceful life shattered
By the earthly lightning
Discharged by the men of helmet and breastplate
Who loved their neighbors
But not these aliens
Who covered their bodies with colored feathers
Instead of armor like the Spanish knights.)

II

La Marcha Heroica

Las fatigadas naves
pliegan alas de lona. Arpas de cuerdas
resuenan con el viento.
Atraviesan las anclas
los hondos aposentos cristalinos
hasta morder el fondo. Marineros
en ágiles maniobras
desembarcan las armas y los fardos,
los toneles que ruedan en la arena,
estandartes y cruces
que las aves marítimas saludan
con sus agrios chillidos agoreros.

Las casas de madera les dan la bienvenida
a los desalentados navegantes
que traen en su rostro
el sello de la sombra y la tormenta.
Un grupo cortesano portando el estandarte
del rey sale a la playa a recibir la Flota.
Es la gente leal a la talega
y algunos capitanes y señores
de los pueblos vecinos que se suman
al Pacificador para su empresa
contra el Primer Tirano de las Indias.

¡Oh ejército errabundo
de lanceros, marinos, eclesiásticos,
de caballeros y de labradores
por la cálida costa ecuatorial
imperio de los loros
en verdes y pacíficas bandadas,
vegetación volante
sobre el fértil engaño de la selva

II

THE HEROIC MARCH

The wearied ships
Fold their canvas wings. Harps of cordage
Hum in the wind.
Anchors cross
The deep crystaline caverns
Until they bite the bottom. The sailors
Skillfully maneuvering,
Disembark arms, bundles,
Casks rolled over sand
Standards and crucifixes, saluted
By the shrill cries
Of prophetic seabirds.

The wooden houses welcome
The exhausted travellors,
Wearing on their faces the imprint
Of tempest and darkness.
A group of courtiers carrying the king's standard
Sallies out to the beach to receive the fleet,
The folk loyal to moneypower
And a few captains and gentlemen
Of the nearby villages who are joining
The Peacemaker in his campaign
Against the First Tyrant of the Indies.

Oh army of wanderers
Of lancers, sailors, ecclesiastics,
Oh horsemen and workmen,
Along the humid equatorial coastline,
Kingdom of parrots
In peaceful green bands,
Flying foliage
Above the fertile deception of the forest

donde cada manglar es una trampa
y el pantano, temblante sepultura!

Portoviejo le ofrece sus portales de sombra
al Pacificador. No hay quien levante
la espada contra el clérigo. En su mesa
el trópico amontona
su deleitosa munición pintada:
el melón, la sandía
son balas de cañón que disparó el verano
contra la sed. Los hombres abandonan
su armadura y respiran
mirando al horizonte
en espera paciente de las naves,
invencibles castillos del océano
para el viaje hacia el sur de sangre y oro,
dominio fantasmal de Gonzalo Pizarro.

Otra vez el camino de las olas,
la inmensidad azul que se reparten
delfines y gaviotas,
el bostezo infinito
de los días iguales
llenos de mar y cielo.

Mar recién descubierto donde vagan
las sombras de otras naves que surcaron
por vez primera su extensión ignota.
Días sin viento, inmóviles,
casi sin aire, como estatuas huecas
de oro solar. Los mástiles
con sus fláccidas velas
son astas de estandartes en derrota.
Iza bandera blanca
La Flota ante el espacio
anunciador de muerte.

Where each mangrove clump is a trap
And the swamp a trembling sepulchre!

Portoviejo offers its dark portals
To the Peacemaker. There is no one to
Raise a sword against the cleric. For his table
The tropics heap up
Their delicious painted ammunition:
Spanish melons, watermelons
Are cannonballs which summer discharges
Against thirst. The men shed their armor
And breath deeply,
Gazing at the horizon,
Patiently awaiting the ships,
The invincible castles of the sea,
To make the trip to the golden and bloody south,
The fantasmagoric dominion of Gonzalo Pizarro.

Once more the pathway through the waves,
The blue immensity shared by
Dolphins and seagulls,
The infinite yawn
Of days all alike,
Filled with see and sky.

Newly discovered sea on which float
The shadows of other ships which plowed
Its unknown distances for the first time.
Windless days, motionless,
Almost airless, like hollow statues
Of solar gold. The masts
With their flaccid sails
Are flagpoles for pennants of defeat.
The fleet hoists
A white banner to space,
The herald of death.

Mas un día, de pronto, el viento oceánico
vuelve de sus lejanas correrías
y da impulso a las naves
que su marcha apresuran
frente a costas extrañas
—desértica Península de Santa Elena, tierra
de pozos y de ídolos,
collar de islas del Golfo, gemas fértiles—
hasta llegar a Tumbes, legendaria
Ciudad del Oro, hoy puerto
de vetustos maderos carcomidos
por las aguas más negras que la noche,
Toda la carga puesta en tierrra firme,
los caballos de guerra,
máquinas, armaduras y miles de soldados
y hasta las baterías de las naves,
comienza la gran marcha
por la región de arena
y luego por los bosques intrincados,
por las cumbres con rocas
que guardan el secreto
de oscuros precipicios.

Jauja pródiga, Jauja la florida,
sabrosa en frutos, rica de ganados,
se asoma al horizonte
y en loor de los héroes leales
echa a volar palomas y campanas.
El Pacificador acampa en ese valle.
No hay cuartel general mejor que Jauja:
vive el sol encerrado
en antiguos graneros de maíz,
convertido en millones de fragmentos nutricios.
Terrestre paraíso de soldados
que pasan el invierno
sitiados por las grises hordas de la tormenta.

But suddenly one day the oceanic wind
Returns again from its distant excursions
And moves the ships
Till they sail rapidly
Along strange coasts —
The desert peninsula of St. Helena, land
Of wells and idols,
Necklace of gulf islands, fertile gems —
Until they reach Tumbes, legendary
City of Gold, now a port
Of ancient planking, cancered
By waters darker than night.
All the cargo unloaded on dry land,
The warhorses
The machines, armament for thousands of soldiers,
And even the ships' batteries;
The long march begins
Through sandy regions
And then through tangled forests,
Over the peaks of cliffs
Guarding the secrets
Of obscure precipices.

Prodigal Jauja, blossoming Jauja,
Luscious with fruit, rich in cattle,
Rises up on the horizon
And in praise of the loyalist heroes
Sets flying its pigeons and bells.
The Peacemaker encamps in this valley,
No better barracks than Jauja:
The sun lives imprisoned
In the ancient corn granaries
Converted into millions of nourishing particles,
A paradisal land for soldiers
Who pass the winter besieged
By the grey hordes of tempests.

Después, meses de marcha cual siglos de fatiga
por los malos caminos.
Los hombres gesticulan, se despeñan
fantoches de cansancio en telones de polvo,
títeres remojados en telones de lluvia.
La amenaza constante del barranco
—¡oh diabólico tigre del abismo!—,
la sucesión de niebla,
polvo y lluvia con mantos mendicantes
que escamotean el paisaje entero,
mientras helados vientos emisarios
propagan con silbidos el mortal ultimatum
de las vecinas nieves.

Hay que trepar los montes escarpados,
hay que cruzar el río torrentoso.
¡El río! Sus yeguadas azules se atropellan
con la sonora prisa de su fuga espumosa
hacia su acabamiento en remotas comarcas.
Arboles corpulentos, mil arbustos
proporcionan el mimbre y la madera
para desafiar al cristalino abismo
con un flexible puente
suspendido en el aire,
frágil máquina audaz
que sirve de camino a los cañones,
a los infantes y cabalgaduras
en su paso nocturno a la otra orilla.

Inaudita visión: va por la senda aérea
un desfile de sombras
con sus armas y cruces y estandartes.
Los hombres tambalean, gritan, oran,
los caballos relinchan,
se encabritan de espanto, pierden el equilibrio,
se precipitan en la negra hondura
y perecen rodando entre las rocas.

Afterward, months of marching, centuries of exhaustion
By impassible roads,
Men, gesturing, fling themselves down,
Fantoms of weariness in rags of dust,
Puppets steeped in shreds of rain.
The constant threat of the ravines —
Oh diabolic jaguar of the abyss! —
The waves of mist,
Dust and rain with beggars' cloaks
That hide the entire landscape
While freezing winds as envoys
Whistle the deadly ultimatum
Of the approaching snow.

There are battlements of mountains to scale.
There are torrential rivers to cross.
The river! Its blue stallions gallop off
With the noisy speed of their foaming flight
To a termination in distant regions.
Thick trees, a thousand bushes
Supply the wood and lashings
To defy the crystaline abyss
With a freeswung bridge
Suspended in air,
Fragile and audacious machine,
Serving as a roadway for cannons,
Infantry and cavalry
Passing at night to the other side.

Unimaginable vision: a file of shadows
Crosses over the aerial pathyway
With arms, crucifixes and standards.
The men stagger, shout, pray:
The horses whinny,
Curvet with fear, lose their balance
And fall into the deep darkness,
Perishing, flung from rock to rock.

195

III

EL CAPACETE DE ORO

Pizarro, llegó el día
de ceñir la armadura esmaltada de oro.
Tu caballo castaño se encabrita
impaciente esperando lo cabalgues
y gobiernes su ímpetu
en la postrer jornada hacia la gloria.

Monarca de mentira,
emperador de burlas de un imperio fantasma,
¿de qué te sirve ahora
el metal de las minas de Potosí? La guardia
de ochenta alabarderos
impedir no podrá el paso inexorable
de la Dama de Hueso.

Vano caudillo, escucha: están contados
tus días terrenales. Tu cabeza vacila,
a pesar del fulgor del capacete de oro.
Ya eres solamente un difunto a caballo,
un difunto que cree todavía estar vivo
e imparte sus órdenes de niebla
que luego se disipan en el aire.

Estás solo delante de tus soldados mudos,
estrafalario ejército con sus aliadas huestes
de guerreros indígenas cubiertos de plumajes
— ¡oh terrestre arco iris volandero! —
ejército pomposo con escasos cañones,
mas con recuas de mulas agobiadas
bajo la carga ingente de los ducados de oro.

Pizarro, compareces
en la llanura inmensa del destino
solo con tu fortuna.

III

The Golden Helmet

Pizarro, the day has come
To don the gold-inlaid armor.
Your chestnut horse rears,
Impatiently waiting to join the cavalcade,
You check his momentum
On the last journey in search of glory.

Monarch of lies,
Mock emperor of a realm of fantasy,
Of what use to you now
Is the metal from the mines of Potosi? An escort
Of eighty halbardiers
Can not retard the inexorable footsteps
Of the Charnal Lady.

Vain chieftain, listen: your earthly days
Are numbered. Your head nods from
The brilliant weight of the golden helmet.
You are no more than a dead man on horseback
A dead man believing himself alive,
Giving orders in words of mist
Soon to be dispelled in air.

You are alone at the head of your mute soldiers,
A slovenly army with a host of allies,
Indian warriors covered with feather uniforms —
Oh earthly flying rainboy —
Pretentious army with but few cannons,
Composed mostly of frightened pack mules
Beneath an enormous cargo of golden ducats.

Pizarro, you appear
Upon the immense plains of destiny
Alone with your fortune.

¿Dónde está tu enemigo? ¿Es acaso esa nube
que baja de los Andes
conducida por Pedro de La Gasca,
el Pacificador de sayal y breviario,
por obispos y frailes misioneros?
Esa nube sonora de plegarias y cánticos,
de cruces y de espadas
se acerca lentamente: es la conciencia,
que crece como sombra de Dios en la llanura.

Frente a tu juez te encuentras impotente,
fingido emperador del Nuevo Mundo
y esperas el mandato supremo, rienda en mano,
clavado en tu montura, los pies en los estribos,
mientras pueblan tu mente las visiones
de tu reino de espanto
fundado sobre ríos de sangre. Entre las rocas
hace su mueca última la cabeza cortada
del anciano Virrey Blasco Núñez de Vela
y surgen los cadáveres de sus cien caballeros
por ti sacrificados. Mira el río,
que parece arrastrar miles de ojos llorosos
de mujeres y niños. ¿Por qué tiemblas
al ver esa figura de infante estrangulado?
Es tu propia simiente maldita. Ya estás solo
hasta el fin de los siglos. Nadie, nadie
perpetuará tu nombre.
Proscrito de la tierra y de los cielos,
Tirano solitario,
tu vestimenta regia es tu mortaja,
y eres, con tus inútiles tesoros,
un humano despojo lamentable,
fatídico ornamento del cadalso.

Día frío, inmutable como un estanque de oro.
Sopla un aire glacial venido de las tumbas.

Where is your enemy? Is it perhaps this cloud
That descends from the Andes
Led by Pedro de La Gasca,
The Peacemaker, with sackcloth and breviary,
With bishops and missionary friars?
The echoing cloud of prayers and hymns,
Of crucifixes and swords
Approaches slowly. It is conscience
Growing like the shadow of God on the plains.

Faced with your judge you find yourself powerless,
Fictitious emperor of the New World,
You await the supreme mandate, your hand on the reins,
Fixed in your saddle, feet in the stirrups,
Your mind peopled with visions
Of your reign of terror,
Product of rivers of blood, Among the cliffs
The severed head of the former Viceroy, Nuñez de Vela,
Appears with its last grimace and there rise up
the corpses of his hundred knights
Whom you sacrificed. Stare at the river,
It seems to run with thousands of weeping eyes
Of women and children. Why do you tremble
At the face of that strangled infant:
It is your own cursed seed. You are alone
Until the end of the centuries. No one, no one
Will perpetuate your name.
Prescribed on earth and in the heavens,
Solitary tyrant,
Your regal vestment is your shroud,
And you with your useless treasures
Are wretched human refuse,
Sinister ornament for a gallows.

A cold day, motionless as a pool of gold.
A glacial wind blows from out of the tombs.

Los soldados apenas pueden asir las lanzas
con sus heladas manos. Aquí en esta llanura
fue quemado en la hoguera por los conquistadores
el gran Calicuchima
que invocó entre las llamas la justicia del sol.
Ahora, con su dedo de oro te señala
el mismo sol, Pizarro
como al reo mayor del Nuevo Mundo.

Extraña escaramuza del destino
en el vasto escenario
encerrado entre altísimas montañas:
Jaquijaguana, verde bostezo de los Andes.
La legión de la Guerra Sagrada se aproxima
con marcha inexorable.
Su artillería truena como voz de las cumbres
e inflama la llanura:
elocuencia de hierro y fuego que convence
a los amilanados escuadrones
del Traidor que clavó su estandarte rebelde
sobre las tierras vírgenes de América.

Capitanes de atuendos vistosos en sus jacas,
Cepeda, Garcilaso
y luego arcabuceros en columnas
se pasan a las tropas de La Gasca.
Y la caballería en airoso galope
se entrega al enemigo. Las huestes emplumadas
de los indios aliados huyen hacia los montes.
Aterrados los hombres de Pizarro
siguen su ejemplo o corren a rendirse.
Es la derrota incontenible. Solo
cruza el caudillo el campo
y va a entregar su espada al Hombre de la Ley,
al Pacificador del Nuevo Mundo.
Frente a frente se encuentran el Tirano,

The soldiers can scarcely hold their lances
With frozen hands. Here upon the plains
The Great Calicuchima
Was burnt at the stake by the conquistadores;
From the flames he called upon the sun for justice.
Now with its golden finger the same sun
Points to you, Pizarro,
The greatest criminal of the New World.

Strange, fateful skirmish
In the vast theatre
Enclosed by the highest mountains:
Jaquijaguana, green yawn of the Andes.
The legion of the Holy War approaches
With inexorable tread.
Its artillery thunders like the voice of the summits
And kindles the plains:
The eloquence of iron and fire convinces
The terrified squadrons
Of the Traitor who set up his rebel standard
Upon the virgin lands of America.

Captains with imposing garments, on their warhorses,
Cepeda, Garcilaso,
And then crossbowmen in columns
Cross over to the troops of La Gasca.
And the cavalry at a smart gallop
Deserts to the enemy. The plumed hordes
Of the Indian allies fly to the mountains.
In terror Pizarro's men
Follow their example or run to surrender.
It is an unrestrainable rout. Alone
The chieftain ccrosses the field of battle
And gives up his sword to the Man of the Law,
The Peacemaker of the New World.
Face to face they meet, the tyrant,

ya la cabeza libre del capacete de oro,
y el clérigo que supo
con un arma invisible, la palabra,
vencer a su enemigo. Frente a frente,
el emisario de la vida eterna
y Gonzalo Pizarro, rey sin reino,
capitán sin soldados,
aliado sin ventura de la muerte,
potentado del único tesoro: su sepulcro.

His head now bare of the golden helmet,
And the cleric who knew how to overthrow
His army with an invisible weapon,
The word. Face to face
The emissary of eternal life
And Gonzalo Pizarro, king without kingdom,
Captain without soldiers,
Luckless ally of death,
Possessor of a single treasure: his own tomb.

EL ALBA LLAMA A LA PUERTA
1965-1966

JORNADA EXISTENCIAL

¡Oh reino inencontrable, Florida o Eldorado!
No hay rastro entre las rocas
de la Fuente de Eterna Juventud ni del oro
sobre la piel desnuda del monarca.
He buscado sin tregua
el indicio celeste en la corteza de árbol,
la escritura en la nube,
sin dar con el camino del reino suspirado.

El arado del sol ara mi frente
en labranza de días y de años sucesivos.
Jornadas de la sed,
deslumbrada por altos espejismos
de aguas inexistentes
para la travesía del desierto.

Derrotero escondido,
gasté mis días en buscarte en vano
por intrincados bosques,
por países de piedras y de arena,
por ciudades inmensas como selvas en llamas.

El polvo de oro se aventó en el aire.
Los labios de la arena agotaron la fuente.
Me revela el ocaso su secreto:
El país de Eldorado está en nosotros mismos.
Imperio de las flores y delicias
regido por el hombre, rey desnudo.
Soy el descubridor de la región postrera,
conquistador del reino efímero sin nombre
en las fronteras últimas
del viento y de la noche.

EXISTENTIAL JOURNEY

Oh never-t-be-encountered kingdom, Florida or Eldorado!
Among the rocks there is no trace
Of the Fountain of Eternal Youth nor the gold
Adorning the monarch's naked skin.
I have sought ceaselessly
For the celestial sign in the bark of a tree,
The writing on the cloud,
Without hitting upon the road to the longed-for kingdom.

The plow of the sun furrows my forehead
In daily toil, year after year.
Days of thirst
Gleaming with mirages from the sky
Of non-existent waters
For crossing the desert.

Hidden route,
I waste my days seeking you in vain
Through intricate forests,
Through countries of stone and sand
Through immense cities like woods in flames.

Golden dust billowed in the air.
Lips of sand dried up the fountain.
The sunset reveals its secret to me:
The country of Eldorado is within ourselves.
Empire of flowers and delights
Ruled by the man, the naked king.
I am the discoverer of the ultimate region,
Conquistador of the nameless ephemeral kingdom
On the last frontiers
Of wind and of night.

LA MINA MAS ALTA

El día descubre al fin
las minas de oro del cielo.
No hay Eldorado más puro
que el de ese altísimo reino.

Jinetes de hierro y vidrio
me miran desde los techos,
centinelas de un tesoro
que es una cueva de fuego.

Cielo, en vano cada día
me revelas tu secreto:
Eldorado inalcanzable,
mina de nubes y sueños.

THE LOFTIEST MINE

The day finally discloses
The gold mines of the sky.
There is no purer Eldorado
Than this highest kingdom of all.

Horsemen of iron and glass
Stare at me from rooftops,
Guardian of a treasure
Which is a cave of fire.

Sky, vainly each day
You reveal your secret to me:
Unattainable Eldorado,
Mine of clouds and dreams.

DESCUBRIMIENTO

Navego cada noche rumbo al día.
En cada amanecer descubro un nuevo mundo,
una América virgen
poblada de una flora y fauna de prodigio.

Miro por vez primera las cosas inauditas
entre los colibríes de la aurora.
Me rodean las tribus inocentes.
En mi ventana vuela el pájaro totémico.

A cada paso encuentro el mineral precioso.
Fundo una población en el desierto.
Mi armadura me vuelve invulnerable
a las flechas del día.

Explorador, colono de la sombra,
vadeo grandes ríos.
Me reciben naciones con tributos
aún más deslumbrantes que el ocaso.

Mujer, ¡oh prisonera!
en mi descubrimiento cotidiano del mundo:
hay más oro en tu pelo
que en los viejos galeones de las Indias.

Cada día acumulo mi tesoro
y en la noche navego
con rumbo a un Continente
nunca antes descubierto.

DISCOVERY

Each night I journey toward day.
I discover a new world in each dawn,
A virgin America
Peopled with prodigious fauna and flora.

For the first time I behold unheard of things
Among the hummingbirds of dawn.
I am surrounded by innocent tribes.
The totemic bird flies into my window.

At each step I discover a precious gem
I founded cities in the desert.
My armor keeps me invulnerable
By the arrows of day.

Explorer, colonizer of darkness,
I ford great rivers
Nations receive me with tribute
Far more dazzling than the sunset.

Oh woman, prisoner
Of my quotidian discovery of the world:
The golden treasure in your skin
Exceeds that carried in the old galleons from the Indies.

Each day I accumulate my riches
And at night I set sail
Toward a Continent
Never seen before.

YO SOY EL BOSQUE

Me interrogo en la noche americana
bajo constelaciones que me miran
con sus ojos de puma:
¿Quién soy, en fin de cuentas? ¿Yo soy el navegante
que descubrió las tierras y los ríos,
trazó el surco, sembró la primera semilla,
fundó pueblos, ciudades y naciones?
¿Soy el hombre que ardió sobre la leña
antes que revelar los tesoros ocultos?
¿Yo levanté la cúpula de piedra,
labré, esculpí, doré la madera sagrada,
hice surgir del seno de la arcilla
todo un mundo animado?

¿Soy el hombre del gremio
que se lanzó a la fiesta de la pólvora
frente al adusto coro de fusiles
para mirar la imagen más limpia de su pueblo?
Yo cambio de vestido según las estaciones,
los climas, las edades, los países;
pero soy siempre el mismo:
lo delata mi frente repleta de universo.

Descifré entre los astros
las noticias del cosmos,
recorrí el laberinto de los libros
hasta encontrar la toga
y tu luz inmortal, sabiduría;
mas todo lo perdí un domingo en el bosque
cuando el rocío me explicó llorando
que la tierra es el reino de lo efímero.

¿Soy hombre de navíos y toneles,
orfebre, campesino, ebanista de sombras,

I AM THE FOREST

I ask myself, in the American night
Under constellations which stare at me
With their puma's eyes:
Who am I, after all? Am I the navigator
Who discovered the fields and rivers,
Traced the furrow, sowed the first seed,
Founded towns, cities and nations?
Am I the man who burned above the pyre
Rather than reveal hidden treasures?
Did I raise the stone cupola,
Shape, carve gild the sacred wood,
Make a whole living world
Spring from the breast of the clay?

Am I the man of the guild
Who flung himself into the fiesta of gunpowder
Faced the stern file of rifles
To envidage a cleaner image of his people?
I change my clothes with the seasons,
The climates, ages, countries:
But I am always the same
My forehead proclaims it, full of universe.

I deciphered the news of the cosmos
Among the stars,
I traversed the labyrinth of books
Until I encountered the toga
And your immortal light, wisdom;
But I lost all this one Sunday in the forest
When the dew explained to me with tears
That the earth is the transitory kingdom.

Am I a man of ships and barrels,
Jewelry-maker, peasant, carpenter of shadows,

peregrino del mundo,
novicio que pasea sus sueños en el claustro?
Soy todos a la vez en invisible suma:
un filósofo griego, un joven de Bizancio
se dan la mano en la plaza de mi alma.
con un rebelde, un monje,
un árabe sensual, un castellano recio
y un astrónomo indio de mi América.
Yo soy un hombre-pueblo, un hombre sucesivo
que viene desde el ser original
hasta formar la suma: un hombre solo.

Epocas ataviadas con sus cambiantes trajes,
el diverso color de los países,
todas las religiones y los mitos
forman mi patrimonio,
y mi mano sostiene al mismo tiempo el libro
y la flecha que vuela.
Soy el reo y el juez, el verdugo y el mártir,
el hombre de cien máscaras.
Plural y a la vez único,
soy el hombre del bosque y soy el bosque mismo.

Pilgrim of the world,
Novice who paces out his dreams in a cloister?
I am all at the same time, invisible summation:
A Greek philosopher, a youth of Byzantium
Grip each other's hands in the place of my soul,
With a rebel, a monk.
A sensual Arab, a stiff-necked Spaniard
And an Indian astronomer of my America.
I am a man-people, a successive man
Who descends from the original being
To become the summation, a single man.

Epochs, costumed with changing dress,
The diverse colors of countries,
All religions and myths
Form my patrimony,
And my hand holds at one time the book
And the flying arrow.
I am the judge and accused, the executioner and the martyr
The man of hundred masks,
Plural and at the time single,
I am the man of the forest and I am the forest itself.

FANTASMA DE LAS GRANJAS

Mi sombra penetrada por los pastos con rocío,
por las constelaciones prisioneras en las granjas,
por la respiración de los hombres dormidos
en sus tumbas provisionales,
avanza hasta el camino descubridor de horizontes.
La angustia cósmica de las ranas me atraviesa.
Las ranas metafísicas dialogan con los astros.
Cada rana, monedero del silencio,
pierde una a una
sus monedas de cobre.

El río desnudo baja de la montaña
como un arcángel con su armadura de cristal.
Escucha: el caballo levanta su casco herrado
y lo hunde en el agua de los sueños
con lentitud semejante a la danza.

Tierra amada: te siento vivir dentro de mí
con la totalidad de tus formas y seres.
El rumor de tus árboles circula entre mis huesos.
Mientras todo duerme
laboro como una abeja en las colmenas del espíritu.

A DREAM OF FARMHOUSES

My shadow, penetrated by dewy pastures,
By constellations imprisoned in farmhouses,
By the breathing of sleeping men
In their temporary tombs,
Advances on the road which leads to horizons.
The cosmic anguish of frogs pierces me.
Metaphysical frogs converse with the stars,
Each frog, coiner of silence
Loses its coppers
One by one.

The naked river beneath the mountain,
Like an archangel armored in crystal,
Listens: the horse lifts its iron hoof
And plunges it into the water of dreams
With the slow movements of the dance.

Beloved land! I feel you living within me
Full of the sum of your shapes and beings.
The murmur of your trees flows among my bones.
While all is sleeping,
I work like a bee in the hive of the spirit.

ESTACIÓN PENÚLTIMA

A mi vuelta de exóticos países,
después de cada viaje
mis lágrimas derramo como Ulises.

En su gran recipiente de cristal, la ventana
me ofrece el mundo entero
desde el cielo oriental de porcelana

hasta el trigal cristiano panadero,
las lanzas del maíz americano
y el campo universal con su sendero.

Inútil viaje. Vuelta inoportuna:
suspiro como Ulises
por la Ítaca celeste de la luna.

THE LAST STATION

Returning from exotic countries,
After each voyage,
Like Ulysses my tears fall.

In its great crystal cup, the window
Offers me the whole world,
From the sky of oriental porcelain.

To the Christian baker, the wheatfield,
The lances of American corn
And the universal countryside with its pathway.

A useless voyage. An inopportune return:
Like Ulysses I sigh
For the celestial Ithaca of the moon.

NO HAY

En las librerías no hay libros,
en los libros no hay palabras,
en las palabras no hay esencia:
hay sólo cáscaras.

Lienzos pintados y fetiches
hay en los museos y salas.
En la Academia hay sólo discos
para las más furiosas danzas.

En las bocas hay sólo humo,
en los ojos sólo distancias.
Hay un tambor en cada oído.
En la mente bosteza el Sáhara.

Nada nos libra del desierto.
Del tambor nada nos salva.
Libros pintados se deshojan,
leves cáscaras de la Nada.

In the bookstores there are no books,
In the books there are no words,
In the words there is no essence:
There are only husks.

There are painted canvasses and fetiches
In museums and halls.
In the Academy there are only
Recordings for the wildest dances.

In mouths there is only smoke,
In eyes only distances.
There is a drum in each ear.
The Sahara yawns in the mind.

Nothing frees us from the desert.
Nothing saves us from the drum.
Painted books shed their pages,
Frails husks of Nothing.

ISLAS NIPONAS

Tomo con los palillos un corazón enano
entre granos de arroz que ríen con sus dientes minúsculos
a la sombra de los pinos marítimos
que vieron llegar por las olas la estatua del dios
y por las nubes la barca del hombre
fundador de dinastías.

Los sacerdotes de cabeza rapada
llevan el dosel del cielo
cerca del templo de laca
vacío hasta las lágrimas de cera.
Los santos hombres de Zen se refugian en un islote
para ver la caída de la hoja,
lengua de lo alto.

Los mendigos engañan su hambre tocando la flauta.
Al ocaso, el sol mira de reojo
las ventas de pescado momificado.
La luces de Ginza tiemblan en la red de las constelaciones,
mientras las anguilas recorren la tierra
en busca de los lagos nupciales.
Ningunos ojos más llenos de amor humano
que los de la joven manchú sobre las esteras
ante el cuerpo del extranjero comprador de caricias.

Kioto, Kamakura, Karuizawa:
miles de años han madurado la civilización de madera
contemplada con una sonrisa enigmática
por la inmensa estatua del dios de bronce
hueco como una campana,
en espera de los tifones océanicos
que dejarán sólo un esqueleto de pez sobre la arena.

With chopsticks I eat a dwarf heart
Among grains of rice laughing with minute teeth
In the shade of pines by the sea
Which have seen the statue of the god arrive on the waves
And through the clouds the ship of the man
Who founded dynasties.

The shaven-headed priests
Raise the canopy of the sky
About the lake temple
Empty except for tears of wax.
The sacred followers of Zen take shelter on an island
To watch the leaf fall,
The tongue of heaven.

Beggars deceive their hunger by playing the flute.
From the west the sun looks askance
Upon markets of mummified fish.
The lights of Ginza tremble in the net of the constellations
While eels traverse the earth
In search of their nuptial lakes.
No eyes are more filled with human love
Than those of the manchu girl upon her mats
Confronting the body of the foreign buyer of caresses.

Kioto, Kamakura, Karuizawa:
Thousand of years have matured a civilization of wood
Contemplated with an anigmatic smile
By the immense statue of the god in bronze,
Hollow as a bell,
That awaits oceanic typhoons
Which leave only a fish skeleton on the sand.

Zen: mira mi mano fláccida. Soy un hombre de Zen.
No tengo otro cuenco de arroz que la luna.
Sin embargo, en mi corazón reverdece la sabiduría
como un limonero enano
y en mi paladar se redondea la palabra
antes de salir a deshacerse en el aire.

Zen: behold my relaxed hand. I am a follower of Zen.
I have no rice bowl other than the moon.
And yet, in my heart wisdom sprouts
Like a dwarf lemon tree
And in my throat the word takes shape
Before it emerges to dissolve in the air.

LES HALLES

Camiones repletos de violetas,
mojados de lluvia y cantos de gallos,
entran por las puertas de Paris todas las madrugadas
sembrando lunas y relámpagos en los charcos,
y salen por las mismas puertas en pleno día
colmados de sombra,
después de abandonar sobre las aceras
su cargamento de campo amasado con sol.
Llevadme, camiones enmohecidos,
al paraíso de la cebolla y las trenzas rubias
donde yo pueda lavar mis ojos
para ver un mundo enjoyado de rocío.

Pesad, pesad el pescado y las lechugas,
pesad la luna entera,
pesad los corazones azucarados por libras,
las lágrimas por litros,
pesad una ensalada de sueños,
sacad de los camiones todo el amor del mundo,
toda la carga pura
preparada por meses de trabajo
y por la paciencia fecundante del agua.

La cigüeña del aceite picotea la luna,
cuando las sombras devoran los últimos caballos blancos.
Digo cigüeña: mi mente responde estaño,
mientras un río relumbra en la ventana
sin poder entrar.

Todas las plumas
de la luna y la cigüeña
caben en la funda de la nube
durante varios días.
Después, las plumas caen y es el invierno.

LES HALLES

CENTRAL MARKET OF PARIS

Trucks full of violets,
Wet with rain and the crowing of cocks,
Enter the gates of Paris each day at dawn
Sowing moons and lightnings in pools,
And leave by the same gates at midday,
Heaped with shadow,
After leaving behind upon the sidewalks
Their cargoes of country kneaded with sunlight.
Carry me, mouldy trucks,
To the paradise of the onion and the blond braids
Where I may bathe my eyes
In the vision of a world jewelled with dew.

Weigh, weigh the fish and the lettuce:
Weigh the whole moon,
Weigh sweetened hearts in pounds,
Tears in liters;
Weigh a salad of dreams,
Take from the trucks all the love of the world
All that pure freight
Prepared by months of labor
And the fertilizing patience of water.

The stork of oil pecks at the moon,
When the shadows devour the last white horses.
Oh region of dew,
Beyond those roads which lead
To the final frontier guarded by the crows.

All the feathers
Of the moon and the stork
Fit into the envelope of the cloud
For a number of days.
Afterwards the feathers fall and it is winter.

Listo para el asador
se vende el invierno ya desplumado.
El vino del crepúsculo en las remolachas
alarma la inocencia de la lechuga,
hermana mayor de la rosa.
¡Oh repollo! linaje del suelo
bendecido por la lluvia:
las cabezas de la familia real conducida en la carreta
al último suplicio
caerán en el saco.

Camiones, grandes cofres de lona
repletos de viento:
llevadme a la comarca escondida
donde nunca mueren las hojas,
junto al agua que refleja un rostro inocente
entre legumbres redondas como la luna;
¡oh comarca de rocío,
fuera de las rutas que conducen
a la frontera final guardada por los cuervos!

Ready to be roasted,
Winter is sold, already plucked.
Twilight wine in the beets
Alarms the innocence of the lettuce,
Sister of the rose,
Oh Cabbage, of earthly lineage
Blessed by the rain:
The heads of the royal family carried in the car
At the final punishment
Will fall in the sack.

Trucks, great coffers of canvas
Full of wind:
Carry me to that hidden region
Where the leaves never die,
Near the water reflecting an innocent face,
Among vegetables round as the moon;
Oh region of dew,
Beyond the road which leads
To the last frontier guarded by the crows!

HUMBOLDT

Las alturas de América recorriste en tu mula,
¡oh Capitán, más grande que los conquistadores!
hollaste los volcanes hasta encontrar el fuego
de la verdad telúrica.
Nuevo descubridor del mundo americano
en pájaros y plantas, animales y piedras,
descifraste el lenguaje del hombre natural
aliado del relámpago y del alba,
del salto del jaguar y del lago dormido.

Encontraste las huellas de las viejas culturas
olvidadas en medio de la selva
o cerca de las nubes en los riscos andinos.
Subiste a dialogar entre las fumarolas
con el dios escondido en el cáliz volcánico
de pistilos de fuego
y encontraste la roca y la hoja de banano
cubiertas de escritura misteriosa.
Enseñaste a leer los raros signos
pintados con el zumo de las frutas
y sangre de los pájaros.

Comprendiste la forma de las ruinas
de palacios y tumbas de monarcas
que observaban el curso de los astros,
gobernaban su pueblo con un amor de padres
y hablaban la verdad sin temor a la muerte.

Humboldt, amigo de los hombres libres,
inspirador de mártires y de héroes,
liberador de pueblos,
precursor de Bolívar,
el cazador de águilas.
Al paso de tu mula

You traversed the heights of America on your mule,
Oh Captain, greater than the conquistadors!
You entered volcanos to reach the fires
Of teluric truth.
You discovered the American world anew
In plants and birds, in beasts and stones
And deciphered the language of the aboriginal man
Ally of the lightning and the sunrise,
Of the jaguar's leap and the sleeping lake.

You came upon the traces of old cultures
Long forgotten in the depths of the forest,
Or, close to the clouds and the Andeam peaks,
You climbed to converse with fuming craters,
Hidden gods in the calix of the volcano
With its fiery pistils,
And you gazed upon the mysterious writing
Which covers the rock and the banana leaf.
You learned how to read the strange signs
Painted with the juice of fruits
And the blood of birds.

You understood the shapes of ruins.
Palaces and tombs, left by rulers
Who observed the orbits of stars,
Governed their peoples with a father's love
And spoke the truth without fear of death.

Humboldt, lover of free people,
Inspirer of martyrs and heroes,
Liberator of peoples
And herald of Bolívar,
The huntsman of eagles.
The hoofbeat of your mule

despertaste países,
forjaste un mundo nuevo
y alzaste el estandarte de la luz
en la noche de siglos.

Awakened nations,
You forged a new world
And raised the standard of light
In the night of the centuries.

TRANSFIGURACIÓN DE LA LLUVIA

La lluvia de cabellos dorados por el sol
llega hasta mis manos con sus alas mojadas.
Me cubre con su gran beso de niña difunta.
Lluvia que resbalas con tu cuerpo transparente,
deja caer tus sucesivas túnicas
y tiéndete en el suelo como una virgen de cristal.
Haz correr tus lágrimas en las ventanas.
Sueña cantando, ¡oh reina sombría!
entre las columnas y los juncos de tu reino.
Mueve los títeres terrestres con tus cordeles líquidos.
Sembradora venida del cielo,
arroja tus semillas y flores que se deshacen.
Encierra al hombre en tu inmensa jaula de vidrio,
tu océano vertical que sepulta las cosas.
En memoria de tu paso,
refúgiate en el hongo fugaz de una burbuja
durante miles de años
hasta ser un eterno ojo de piedra.

TRANSFIGURATION OF THE RAIN

Rain with hair gilded by the sun
Reaches my hands with its wet wings.
It covers me with its great kiss of a lifeless girl.
Rain, gliding with your transparent body,
Let fall your successive tunics
And stretch out on the ground like a crystal virgin.
Let your tears fall on windows,
Ring with song, oh dusky queen,
Among the columns and rushes of your kingdom!
Move terrestrial puppets with your liquid strings.
Sower, come from the sky,
Scatter your seeds and disappearing flowers.
Enclose man in your immense glass cage,
Your vertical ocean which buries everything.
In memory of your passing,
Take refuge in the fleeting mushroom of a bubble
For thousands of years
Until you become an eternal eye of stone.

AGUA GERMINAL

La raíz de plata del relámpago
une el árbol del cielo con la tierra.
Cada trueno es un templo que se desploma.
La tormenta viene desde la Antigüedad,
con su viejo olor de piedra eterna.
Es un recuerdo planetario
que nubla la frente del cielo.
El agua evoca los orígenes,
con su canto elemental
aprendido en las cuevas de la sombra.

Tormenta inmemorial: lava mi frente
con tu onda meteórica,
para que yo pueda ver un mundo limpio
como el que se copió por vez primera
en mis ojos de niño.
Haz germinar la semilla del amor
en mi corazón estéril
por tantos años de viaje
a través del desierto.

The silver root of the lightning
Unites the tree of the sky with the earth.
Each thunderbolt is a temple collapsing.
The tempest comes from Antiquity
With its ancient odor of eternal stone.
It is a planetary memory
Which clouds the front of the sky.
Water evokes origins
With its elemental song
Learned in the caves of darkness.

Immemorial tempest: wash my forehead
With your meteoric wave,
That I may see a world as clean
As that which my childish eyes
Reproduced for the first time.
Make the seed of love germinate
In my heart, parched
By so many years of journeying
Across the desert.

INVOCACIÓN AL AIRE

Te invoco, dios del aire,
el del traje de vidrio
y la corona azul de plumería,
ahora que me siento profundamente urbano,
tan repleto de gente como una plaza pública.

Te invoco, dios del aire,
el de alas transparentes.
Yo, súbdito de un reino anterior a la rueda,
me siento atravesado por miles de automóviles,
como una pista gris en el crepúsculo.

Tú, nutrido de espacio y de suspiros,
dios de plumas azules,
morador solitario de la altura,
cédeme una parcela de tu reino.
Dentro de mi la multitud habita
y ya no tengo sitio para vivir conmigo.

INVOCATION TO THE AIR

I invoke you, god of air,
You, in costume of glass
With a crown of blue feathers,
Now that I feel myself profoundly urban,
As full of people as a public square.

I invoke you, god of air,
You, with transparent wings,
I, subject of a realm preceding the wheel,
Feel myself run over by thousands of automobiles
Like a grey highway in the twilight.

You, nourished by space and sighs,
God of blue feathers,
Solitary dweller in height,
Cede to me a bit of your kingdom.
The multitude lives within me
And I have no room to live with myself.

DIOS DE ALEGRÍA

Dios de alegría:
Te entreví
en pleno día.

La túnica de luz
se enredaba en el árbol
sin memoria de cruz.

Tu paso de cristal
bajaba la escalera
del manantial.

El cielo sonreía.
Iban flor y guijarro
en buena compañía.

Todo era lenguaje
divino.
Cada ala era un viaje

hacia el Dios de alegría,
todo luz.
El mundo ardía.

GOD OF JOY

God of joy,
I glimpsed you
In full day.

The tunic of light
Was enfolding the tree
Without memory of cross.

Your crystal footsteps
Descended the staircase
Of the torrent.

The sky smiled.
Flower and pebble
Were keeping good company.

All was language
Of divinity.
Each wing a journey

Toward the God of joy,
All light.
The world was on fire.

LENGUAS VIVAS

Deja caer el árbol
sus silabas verdes
que traducen
el lenguaje del bosque.

Sabiduría escrita
en las venas de las hojas.
El destino es legible
en las líneas de clorofila.

Una reserva de ternura
esconden las cortezas
de rodillas rugosas,
¡oh ternura en hileras!

La lengua más breve,
al volar por el aire
articula su palabra,
profecía del bosque.

LIVING TONGUES

The tree lets fall
Its green syllables,
As it translates
The speech of the forest.

Wisdom written
In the veins of the leaves.
Destiny can be read
In the lines of chlorophyl.

On their rugged knees
The treetrunks are hiding
A reticent tenderness,
Oh tenderness in rows!

The briefest tongue
As it flies through the air
Speaks the prophetic
Word of the woodland.

DEL « LIBRO DEL DESTIERRO »

II

Higuera: vejez fértil
más que cualquiera juventud frondosa.
A atesorar me enseñas dulzura año por año,
a ofrecer miel secreta
concentración jugosa de crepúsculos
madurando al amparo de las hojas
ilustres por su número enigmático
profusión de verdor hasta la altura
fijada por designios misteriosos.
No puedes crecer más, oh sabia higuera
retorcida por íntima tortura,
pero sobre tu cuerpo contrahecho
sostienes una carga de esperanza
y repartes tu vieja dulcedumbre.

III

El lucero se acerca de puntillas al charco.
No se sabe si va a buscar su moneda perdida.
De pronto desaparece en el agua
y sube al cielo
donde se extravía entre la polvareda de los astros.
¿Todas estas luces para el entierro de mi alma
que está velándose desde hace años
en este armatoste de hueso pensativo?
No queda otro camino que las constelaciones
para llegar al punto de la nada
donde comenzó mi viaje.
Lucero pordiosero:
recoge los millares de monedas dispersas
en el gran charco del cielo.

FROM "THE BOOK OF EXILE"

II

Figtree: old age more potent
Than any leafy youth.
You teach me to hoard sweetness year by year,
To offer a secret honey,
Juicy concentrate of twilights
Maturing under the protection of the leaves
Distinguished for their enigmatic number,
Fixed by mysterious designs,
Profusion of verdure up to the summit,
Oh wise figtree, you can grow no longer,
Twisted by intimate tortures,
But upon your deformed body
You carry a load of hope
And spread your ancient sweetness.

III

The morning star approaches the pool on tiptoe,
We do not know if it is looking for its lost coin.
Suddenly it disappears in the water
And mounts to the sky
Where it goes astray in the dust of the suns.
All these lights for the burial of my soul
That has kept vigil for years
In this cumbersome hulk of reflective bone?
There is no road except that of the constellations
By which to reach the point of nothingness
Where my journey begins.
Mendicant morning star,
Collect your thousands of coins
Lost in the great pool of the sky.

A mí me basta una luciérnaga
para velar mi alma.

IV

Amé nuestro planeta.
Me nutrí de países y de climas.
Yo era fuego encendido en un segundo
era amigo del hombre y del caballo
era la libertad buscando patria,
era la patria andando hasta ser libre.

Era el rocío, hermanos, el rocío
repartiendo la paz entre los hombres
era la paz buscando una morada,
un oasis de plantas en la arena.
Andaba con la luz por todas partes
sin hallar el refugio que buscaba.

Los vegetales eran mi familia
mi palabra era máquina de flores.
Mago de insectos, pájaros y fuentes
compuse con azules materiales
un cielo terrenal para uso propio
y de todos los hombres, mis hermanos.

V

Te reconozco viento del exilio,
saqueador de jardines
errante con tus látigos de polvo.
Me persiguen sin tregua tus silbidos
y borras mis pisadas de extranjero.

To watch over my soul
One firefly is enough.

IV

I have loved our planet,
Countries and climates have nourished me.
I was a fire lasting for a moment,
I was a friend to man and horse,
I was liberty seeking a country,
I was a country seeking to be free.

I was the dew, brothers, the dew
Spreading peace among men.
I was peace seeking a resting place,
And oasis of foliage in the sand.
I bore light everywhere
Without finding the refuge I sought.

I belonged to the family of plants,
My speech was a machine made of flowers.
Magus of insects, birds and fountains,
Out of blue stuff I fashioned
An earthly sky for the personal use
Of all men, my brothers.

V

I recognize you, wind of exile,
Despoiler of gardens,
Rover with whips of dust;
Your whistling follows me ceaselessly
And you wipe out my foreign footsteps.

Te reconozco viento de la augustia
roedor de los árboles.
Propagas el desorden y el estruendo,
me envuelves en tu inmenso torbellino,
manto glacial que intenta ser mortaja.

Me muerdes, fiera cósmica
seguida de tus perros implacables
oh furia del espacio
no cesas en tus coros enemigos,
salteador emboscado en las esquinas
para impedirme el paso hacia el refugio.
Viento de angustia, viento del exilio.

XVIII

En la hogaza de pan hallo la patria
su contenido cálido de intimidad doméstica
su perfume solar igualitario
repartido en blandura protegida
por las manos del pueblo.

En la hogaza de pan veo el semblante
de las madres del mundo
sobre un fondo de campos de maíz y de trigo
ondulante de vida
envueltos en vapores matinales.

Aspiro el pan como una flor dorada.
Palpo su suavidad
de infante del verano fajado en su corteza
de cereal sonante
con memoria de abeja y dalia secas.
En la hogaza de pan hallo mi patria
en un lugar cualquiera del planeta.

I recognize you, wind of anguish,
Rodent of trees.
You sow disorder in the thunder,
You wrap me in your immense vortex,
Glacial cloak intent on becoming shroud.

You are killing me, cosmic carnivore,
Followed by your implacable hounds,
Oh fury of space!
Your hostile choruses never rest,
Leaper from ambush in corners
To prevent me from reaching sanctuary.
Wind of anguish, wind of exile.

XVIII

I discover my native land in the loaf of bread,
Its warm sustance of family intimacy,
Its perfume dispensed, like impartial ground,
With gentle concern
By the hands of the people.

In the loaf of bread I see the face
Of the mothers of the world
Above a landscape of corn and wheat,
Rippling with light
And wrapped in the morning mist.

I breathe in the odor of bread as from a gilded flower,
To my touch it is soft
As the child of spring swaddled in a sheath
Of murmuring grain
With a memory of bees and dried dahlias.
In the load of bread I discover my country
Wherever I happen to be on the planet.

ESTACIONES DE STONY BROOK
A George Quasha

I

Nuevos peldaños
hacia la ventana más alta

Se mira el mundo
dispuesto en trigos y barcos

Abajo el viento
trepa a las más altas ramas

El mar se tiende
orlado de blanco

La claridad más alta
relumbra prisionera
en la ventana límpida.

II

Cuando el verano pasa
con su guitarra de hojas
      la llama de un faisán
        se enciende en la ventana
reviviendo esperanzas extinguidas
de un paraíso oculto
entre las ramas secas.

III

Isla Larga
isla de las ardillas

SEASONS OF STONY BROOK

For George Quasha

I

New steps
to the highest window

The world sees itself
Laid out in wheat and boats

Below the wind
Climbs the highest branches

The sea stretches out
Trimmed with white

The most intense clarity shines
Prisoner
In the clear window.

II

When summer passes
With its guitar of leaves
   The flame of a pheasant
   Burns in the window
Reviving extinguished hopes
Of a hidden paradise
Among dry leaves.

III

Long Island
Island of squirrels

El invierno es una página en blanco
frente a mi ventana
　　Una codorniz
　　cae en la nieve
　　pesado talego
　　de monedas de oro

La Sagrada Biblia está abierta sobre la mesa
en el capítulo de los Salmos.

IV

La ardilla arde en el árbol
El grito del pájaro ayuda a morir al día
La ardilla busca su refugio perdido
La tentación del fruto se interpone en la senda
Poniente rojizo madriguera de ardillas
En el pecho del hombre se oculta
　　una ardilla asustada
La ardilla devora un corazón de cereza
La cola felpuda de la sombra pasa
　　sobre los objetos
En el árbol estremecido
　　arde la ardilla
　　desciende un peldaño
　　baja otra vez
　　aviva su fuego
　　　saltarin
　　limpia el polvo de las hojas
pone en fuga al pájaro que ayuda a morir al día.

V

Despiertan los ojos angélicos de las glicinas
El flautín de vidrio

Winter is a blank page
In front of my window
    A quail
    Falls in the snow
    Heavy bag
    Of golden coins

The Holy Bible is open on the table
At the chapter of Psalms.

IV

The squirrels blazes in the tree
The cry of the bird helps the day to die
The squirrel seeks its lost refuge
The tempration of fruit interposes in the path
Rosy western burrow for squirrels
In man's breast a frightened squirrel
    Hides itself
The squirrel devours a heart of cherry
The bushy tail of the shadow passes
    Over objects
In the quivering tree
    The squirrel blazes
    Goes one step down
    Descends once more
    Revives its fire
      leaping
    It cleans the dust from the leaves
Puts to flight the bird that helps the day to die.

V

The angelic eyes of the wisteria awaken
The glass flute

en el tornasolado
estuche volante
pierde algunas perlas
Los árboles ganan terreno cada día
Los dedos del sol tocan
una por una
todas las flores
El tiempo regresa de su viaje con una sonrisa.

VI

Un ave roja picotea las semillas
oh corazón nutrido de comienzos
Las codornices rehacen una tras otra
las cuentas de un collar ambulante
Cielo y tierra dialogan
La eternidad está presa
en este instante bajo el árbol
Ahora eterno ahora
El horizonte se abre
El viento hincha las velas
¿van a partir sin mí todas las naves?

VII

Dame la bienvenida acantilado
Mar descerraja las puertas de tus sótanos
para dejar pasar cardúmenes de plata
En la cárcel azul
late un pez rojo
único y blando corazón del agua
cruzando soledades
surcadas de relámpagos
En el sueño profundo de las algas
teje y desteje el mar un pensamiento.

In the shifting colors
A flying jewel case
Loses some pearls
The trees win more ground every day
The fingers of the sun touch
All the flowers
One by one
Time returns from its journey with a smile.

VI

A red bird pecks the seeds
A heart nourished by beginnings
The quail one after another
Restring a walking necklace
Earth and sky talk to each other
Eternity is caught
At this moment under the tree
Now eternal now
The horizon opens
The wind fills the sails
Are all the ships going to sail without me?

VII

Cliff, give me a bold welcome
Sea unlock the door of your cellars
To allow shoals of silver to pass
Into the prison of the blue
A red fish thrashes
Single soft heart of water
Crossing solitudes
In the deep sleep of algae
The sea weaves and unweaves a thought.

VIII

Arroyo pedregoso teatro de cristal
donde son personajes
la luciérnaga y el lucero
Agua en la piedra
oh dulzura viajera que se adapta
a la compacta rigidez
de la impasible afirmación inmóvil
        alianza de dos vidas
del reino transparente y del oscuro
        juntos en beneficio
de la planta nutricia y de la sed humana.

IX

Walt Whitman ha venido a visitarme
Miro las barbas de mi viejo amigo
con la gris telaraña de la lluvia
Miro sus botas llenas de barro americano
        En dos sillas de junco
        sentados a la mesa
        gustamos condimentos de palabras
En un rincón cualquiera
        su mirada
hace brotar el tallo de un poema
bordón de caminante
o raíz de hortelano
¿Donde está tu universo? le pregunto
¿Donde el progreso eterno
la victoria
la paz sin amargura?
El agua de la lluvia resbala hasta sus párpados
lágrimas en sus barbas consteladas
Sus hombros se doblegan
        bajo un peso invisible
El moho entra en el pan de las palabras.

VIII

Stony ravine crystal theatre
Where the characters
Are fireflies and bright stars
Water on the rock
Oh passing sweetness which yields
To the impassive montionless affirmation
           Alliance of two lives
Of the transparent kingdom and darkness
           Joined for the benefit
Of plant nutriment and human thirst.

IX

Walt Whitman has come to visit me
I look at the beard of my old friend
With the grey spiderweb of rain
I look at his boots covered with American mud
           In two rush-bottomed chairs
           We sit at the table
           Enjoying condiments of words
In any corner
           His glance
Causes the shoot of a poem to grow
Traveller's staff
Gardner's root
Where is your universe? I ask him
Where is eternal progress
The victory
The peace without bitterness?
The rain drips down to his eyelids
Tears in the constellation of his beard
His shoulders bow
           Beneath the invisible weight
Mould infuses the bread of words.

X

Piedras
           céspedes árboles
           invitan a las nubes
a un festín de claridad
Nacen las velas en el mar: verano
La ira de la espuma
se convierte en remanso
En la tierra el Santo Verdor condenado a la hoguera
entrega su alma al cielo
           Humo de eternidad
           que nadie contempla
De árbol a árbol
tienden lazos invisibles
los vuelos de los pájaros
           Ahora eterno ahora.

X

Stones
>   turf
>   trees invite the clouds
To a luminous festival
Sails are born in the sea: summer
The anger of the foam
Turn into humility
On earth Saint Green condemned to the flames
Gives up his soul to heaven
>   Smoke of eternity
>   Which nobody sees
From tree to tree
Extend invisible bonds
The flight of birds
>   Now eternal now.